The Gospel
in Human
Contexts

The Gospel in Human Contexts

Anthropological Explorations for Contemporary Missions

Paul G. Hiebert

Baker Academic

a division of Baker Publishing Group
Grand Rapids, Michigan

Published by Baker Academic
a division of Baker Publishing Group
P.O. Box 6287, Grand Rapids, MI 49516-6287
www.bakeracademic.com

Printed in the United States of America

Library of Congress Cataloging-in-Publication Data

Hiebert, Paul G., 1932–
    The gospel in human contexts : anthropological explorations for contemporary missions / Paul G. Hiebert.
        p.   cm.
    Includes bibliographical references and index.
    ISBN 978-0-8010-3681-1 (pbk.)
    1. Missions—Theory. 2. Missions—Anthropological aspects. I. Title.
BV2063.H4625 2009
266—dc22   2008056052

Scripture quotations labeled Message are from *The Message* by Eugene H. Peterson, copyright © 1993, 1994, 1995, 2000, 2001, 2002. Used by permission of NavPress Publishing Group. All rights reserved.

Scripture quotations labeled NIV are from the HOLY BIBLE, NEW INTERNATIONAL VERSION®. NIV®. Copyright © 1973, 1978, 1984 by International Bible Society. Used by permission of Zondervan. All rights reserved.

Scripture quotations labeled NRSV are from the New Revised Standard Version of the Bible, copyright © 1989, by the Division of Christian Education of the National Council of the Churches of Christ in the United States of America. Used by permission. All rights reserved.

Scripture quotations labeled RSV are from the Revised Standard Version of the Bible, copyright 1952 [2nd edition, 1971] by the Division of Christian Education of the National Council of the Churches of Christ in the United States of America. Used by permission. All rights reserved.

Contents

Illustrations

Acknowledgments

In the last days of his life, my father scrambled to finish two book manuscripts before mesothelioma, an asbestos-related cancer, claimed his life on this earth in favor of a heavenly walk with my mother and his Lord. (He was looking forward to it.) Trouble with his memory was making it difficult to remember what he had already written, and a continual flow of phone calls and visits from loving family and faithful friends prevented him from accomplishing the task. Fortunately, one of the manuscripts, now in print with Baker Academic under the title *Transforming Worldviews*, was nearly finished apart from the editing, which was ably done by Jeremy Cunningham. The other, this one, was a collection of pieces, some already in print and some written for the occasion. It was intended to be a summary of Dad's thinking about anthropology and missions over the fifty-plus years of his service. A number of us participated in pulling the pieces together. Special mention goes to Linda Hytha, who carefully read and edited the entire manuscript (Emily Davis was her assistant); to Jeffery Wittung, who managed its production; and especially to Jim Kinney, who worked out flexible arrangements with Baker for its publication. My job was to clarify the writing and to watch for duplication, some of which was inevitable in a summary volume such as this one. Every effort was made to put the book into print as Dad intended. Where I have failed at that, I will apologize directly to the author when I myself take that heavenly walk.

Eloise Hiebert Meneses
St. Davids, Pennsylvania
May 27, 2008

Introduction

The Christmas pageant had come to a good end after a rocky start, I thought. There were scenes of the angel addressing Elizabeth, Mary, and Joseph, of Elizabeth's meeting with Mary, and of the birth of Christ. Then the shepherds came on stage, staggering in drunk (in South India shepherds and drunkards are synonymous), followed by a dozen sheep bouncing on all fours and butting one another (all the young children who had no other roles in the play). When the angels of the Lord appeared, they all kneeled, sober and reverent. There were the wise men following the star and, finally, the manger scene as all gathered around the newborn child. The message had gotten through!

Then from behind the curtain leaped Santa Claus, giving gifts to all, the hero of the evening. I was stunned. My first reaction was "Syncretism!"—a mix of Christian and Hindu beliefs. Then I remembered that the missionaries from the West had brought Santa along with Christ. In the West, we have two Christmases. The sacred Christmas centers on the baby Jesus, Mary, Joseph, angels, shepherds, and wise men. It takes place in a warm climate, has palm trees and other tropical plants, sheep, cows and camels, angels, and the star of Bethlehem. The secular Christmas focuses on Santa Claus and elves. It takes place in a cold climate and has evergreen trees, reindeer, sleighs, and the star of the North. We mentally keep the two separate, although we do bring evergreen Christmas trees into the church and mix the two at home. Indian villagers have no supernatural/natural dichotomy and see all these participants as parts of one whole picture. The cultural differences between the missionaries and the villagers had led to a fundamental miscommunication.

As missionaries, pastors, and evangelists, we are involved in complex ministries. To prepare for these, we seek extensive training in Bible schools and seminaries. There, most of the courses focus on exegesis of the Scriptures. Systematic and biblical theologies are at the fore. This training is essential because those who are ministers of the gospel must know it well in order to communicate it effectively. Church history helps us understand the ways Christians have understood the gospel since New Testament times. And we take a few courses on preaching and counseling (Western style). But when we go out in missions, we find that just knowing the gospel in its original context is not enough. We must communicate that gospel to humans who live their everyday lives in worlds far different from our own. Unfortunately we receive little training in the exegesis of human beings and their contexts. At best we may have taken a course on how to learn a new language. Consequently, the gospel we preach goes off into space and does not reach the people we serve (fig. 1).

Figure 1
Bridging the Culture Gap

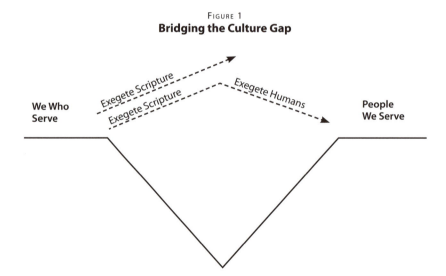

How should we, as missionaries, pastors, and church workers, prepare for our ministries? It is increasingly clear that we must master the skill of human exegesis as well as biblical exegesis to meaningfully communicate the gospel in human contexts. We need to study the social, cultural, psychological, and ecological systems in which humans live in order to communicate the gospel in ways the people we serve understand and believe. Requiring only a course or two on human exegesis is like preparing a doctor by teaching him to put on Band-Aids, stitch wounds, and administer artificial resuscitation. Christian missions and ministries are as complex as medicine and open heart surgery, and, consequently, they require a deep understanding of humans to be effective.

Not only must missionaries and ministers learn how to exegete humans, they must also know how to put the gospel into human contexts so that it is understood properly but does not become captive to these contexts. The gospel is not simply information to be added to current cultural understandings. It is a transforming power that changes individuals and societies into signs and witnesses of the kingdom of God. Moreover we must learn to exegete our own contexts, because these shape the way we understand and communicate the gospel. We often speak of this encounter between gospel and human contexts as indigenization or contextualization.

In this book we look at ways of exegeting human contexts and of communicating the gospel faithfully in these contexts. We argue that this process of communicating the gospel in human settings is a third way of practicing theology, parallel and complementary to systematic and biblical theologies. This third way we call missional theology.

Part 1

Theoretical Foundations

1

Changing Views

How can we embody in human contexts divine revelation given to us in Scripture so that people believe and follow Christ, and societies are transformed? And how can we do this in such a way that the gospel does not become captive to the world? Before we answer these questions, we need to study the way we as Christians have viewed the relationship between the gospel and human contexts.

As humans we live in particular contexts: our family, our neighborhood, our town, our country. We seldom give specific thought to them, but these contexts shape what we see, feel, and value, and what we believe without question to be true, right, and proper. These beliefs are so obvious to us that they seem to be universal. They simply are the way things truly are. We assume that others see things the way we do. Houses have bathrooms, bedrooms, kitchens, and living rooms. Cars are driven on the right side of the road, stay in lanes, and stop at stop signs. We must put postage stamps on letters before dropping them in the mailbox. We fail to recognize that many of the assumptions and values that underlie our culture are not biblically based. They are our human creations.

Most of us, particularly in our childhood, are monocultural. Only when things go wrong, or change rapidly, or when our views of reality conflict with the assumptions from another culture do we question them. Such experiences make us aware that we live in particular contexts, and they force us to start thinking about them—their structure and givens. Others of us have grown up or live in multicultural contexts: missionaries, missionary kids, immigrants, business people, diplomats, and refugees. We are aware of cultural differences and have learned to negotiate between two worlds in daily living. Still, even in these circumstances we often do not stop to consciously examine these contexts, the way they shape our thinking, and the deep differences between them. We are, to some extent, bicultural, but would find it hard to explain to others what this means.

In a rapidly globalizing world, it is important that all of us give thought to human contexts and the way these shape others as well as ourselves. We need to learn how to live in a multicontext world, to build bridges of understanding and relationship between different contexts, and to judge between them. This is true for social, cultural, linguistic, religious, and historical contexts. How do, and how should, we relate to others and to otherness?

As Christians, we are often unaware that our beliefs are frequently shaped more by our culture than by the gospel. We take our Christianity to be biblically based and normative for everyone. We do not stop to ask what parts of it come from our sociocultural and historical contexts, and what parts come from Scripture. Missionaries are forced to deal with sociocultural differences and, therefore, with social and cultural contexts. But even they may take little time to systematically study in depth the contexts in which they serve, despite the fact that the effectiveness of their ministries is determined in large measure by how well they do this.

Finally, humans live in many types of contexts: geographic, social, cultural, political, and historical. Missionaries seek to plant churches in local social contexts and to communicate the gospel in local cultural contexts.[1] The church without the gospel ceases to be the church. The gospel without humans and social institutions, such as families and congregations, dies. In this chapter, we focus primarily on social and cultural contexts and the

---

1. The word *society* as it is used here is defined as the system of relationships that enable people to form communities. The word *culture* is defined as the partially integrated system of ideas, feelings, and values encoded in learned patterns of behavior, signs, products, rituals, beliefs, and worldviews shared by a community of people. Society and culture are subsystems that are part of human realities. Other subsystems include those that are physical, biological, psychological, and spiritual.

importance of understanding them for the sake of missions. A full analysis of missions must take historical, personal, and other contexts into account and examine the relationships among the different contexts in which the people we serve live.

Views of Contextualization

Our conscious awareness of cultural contexts, including our own, often goes through changing perceptions as we encounter others and other-ness. Those who grow up in multicultural settings develop at least some awareness of social and cultural differences and, therefore, of societies and cultures themselves. The changing perceptions outlined below are a model—a way of looking at our growing awareness of others and otherness in cross-cultural ministries. It is not a descriptor of the phases all persons go through in their encounters with other cultures. These changes are not necessarily linear, and they may overlap. Rather, the model is a tool to help us understand the history of the modern mission movement that carried missionaries from Europe and North America to the ends of the earth, and to help us learn from past experiences. Nonetheless, both personal and corporate views of contextualization change as we encounter other cultures and face the questions raised by "otherness."

View One: Noncontextualization

Most monocultural people are largely unaware of the cultures in which they live, or the depth to which these contexts shape how and what they think and do. For them the contextualization of the gospel is not an issue.

NONCONTEXTUALIZATION

"Just go and preach the gospel. Why waste time going to college and seminary?" my boss said when he learned that I wanted to be a missionary and wanted, first, to complete college, seminary, and graduate studies. His is a widespread attitude commonly found in the church.

When people go as missionaries, we know they need to understand the gospel, but we are sure they know enough from church and Sunday school to reach the lost abroad. Even if we recognize their need for more Bible training, most of us are unaware of the profound issues raised by cultural, social, and historical differences. We know that missionaries might benefit from a class or two on the culture in which they plan to serve. We are confident that in a few years they will naturally learn the local language and customs and be able to minister as they have in our church. All they need to do is proclaim the gospel to the people, and the people will understand and believe. They need to persuade the people to leave their old gods and receive Jesus as their Savior, and move on to new areas where the gospel has not been proclaimed. The gospel is seen as acultural and ahistorical in its very nature.

In this phase we equate the gospel with *our* Christianity (fig. 1.1). New converts should learn from us and our ways, and they should join us because we are Christians and this is the way we practice it. To live Christianity differently raises difficult questions. How differently can Christians in other cultures live? Is our Christianity normative for all? To what extent has our way of practicing Christianity been shaped by the gospel, and to what extent by our culture? We avoid these difficult questions and come as outsiders, assuming that new converts will join and imitate us.

The epistemological foundation for this phase is positivism (Hiebert 1999), which holds that our scientific knowledge is an accurate, true photograph of the world and corresponds one-to-one with reality. Its theories are not models but facts. Scientists seek objective truth and must eliminate feelings and morals from the rational/empirical processes used to ascertain truth because they introduce subjectivity—and subjectivity is viewed negatively as contaminating the Truth.

Theological positivism holds that our central concern is truth, and that our theology corresponds one-to-one to Scripture. Other theologies and religions are false and must be refuted. We are concerned with truth and define it in rational terms. We divorce it from feelings and values because these undermine the objectivity of the truth. Our concern is that people

FIGURE 1.1
View One: *Noncontextualization*

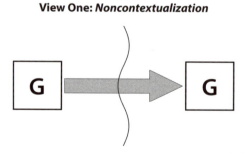

believe the gospel to be truth because *that* determines whether they are saved. We define the truth in propositional terms and seek to transmit it unchanged. We see ourselves as God's lawyers and put our trust in experts who have studied Scripture deeply. Finally, we see the gospel as acultural and ahistorical. It is unchanging and universal, can be codified in abstract rational terms, and can be communicated in all languages without loss of meaning. Neither the sociocultural contexts of the listeners nor that of the messengers need be taken into account.

Most missionaries, when they enter another culture, move quickly to phase two, but some remain in phase one all their lives. They work through translators and control the converts and churches. They make certain that new Christians conform to the cultural norms introduced by the missionary. Converts must wear clothes, learn to read, and have only one wife. They cannot practice theological reflection on their own. They must learn theology from the missionary.

Minimal Contextualization

When we enter another culture, we soon encounter deep differences. We experience culture shock: the feeling of disorientation that arises when all our familiar cultural ways no longer hold. We experience language shock—the inability to communicate even the simplest messages and the growing realization that languages shape the very way we experience and see reality. We also experience religious shock—the fact that other religions make sense to their followers, even though to us these are strange and obviously wrong. We meet Muslims and Hindus who are good people, often better than some of the Christians we know. They can articulate their beliefs clearly and persuasively. How can we say that they are lost? Why are we Christians? Was it a matter of conviction or of birth and upbringing? We are forced to examine our own beliefs more deeply and the basis for our convictions. Such encounters with cultural differences force us to deal with others and, ultimately, with the question of otherness.

This encounter with otherness requires missionaries to decide how they will live in a new land. What kind of food should they eat at home? What kind of clothes should they wear? What kind of houses should they live in? In this stage, missionaries try to preserve their culture abroad for psychological survival and for their children, who, they assume, will eventually return to their home culture.

Otherness also raises the question of the messengers' attitudes toward the local people. They are so different—so other! In this view, we see them as "primitive," "backward," and in need of help to become like us. As we come to know them personally, they become more human to us—friends and neighbors—but we keep a psychological barrier between ourselves and them. They are *others*, not *us*. We do not think seriously of migrating and becoming citizens of the new country or that our children might marry locally and settle down as natives. We think of "returning home" when we retire.

The more we live with and study the people we serve, the more we become aware of the depth and power of their culture and the need to contextualize both the messenger and the message for them to understand and live the gospel. But we are afraid that this contextualization will distort the gospel, so our conclusion is that it must be done minimally (fig. 1.2). We realize that we must speak and translate the Bible into the people's language, and we organize their services and churches in ways the people understand, but we still equate Christianity with our own beliefs and practices.

Figure 1.2
View One-A: *Minimal Contextualization*

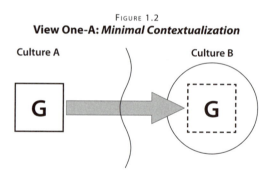

In this paradigm we link Christianity to civilization. We see ourselves as modern and others as primitive and backward—in need of development. Therefore, we do not need to study other cultures deeply, except to find the distortions they cause in understanding the gospel. We build schools and hospitals to teach people the truths of science and to civilize them. We see other cultures as primitive or evil, with little to contribute to our own understanding of reality. There is little in the old culture worth preserving. The minds of the natives are a tabula rasa on which we can write Christianity and science. To become Christian and civilized, the people must become like us. As the Chinese used to say, "One more Christian, one less Chinese."

In positivism signs, such as words and mathematical formulas, are thought to correspond directly to empirical realities (fig. 1.3). The word *tree* refers to real trees, the word *cow* to real cows. This view assumes that

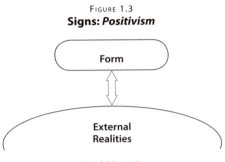

FIGURE 1.3
Signs: *Positivism*

Form

External
Realities

World Outside

all people live in essentially the same world and simply attach different labels to realities. Their thought categories, logic, way of ordering realities, and worldview are essentially like our own, only less developed. In communication and Bible translation, missionaries need simply to find the corresponding words in another language, adjust the grammar, and the people will understand the message accurately.

One characteristic of this view of signs is its strong affirmation of singular truth. Signs are mere labels, but they are directly attached to the truth. So in evangelism and teaching, an emphasis is placed on accurate, rationally developed arguments and apologetic confrontation with other religions. A second characteristic is that communication is measured by what is said or transmitted. It is sender-oriented communication. What is important is the number of sermons preached, hours of radio broadcast, and quantity of tracts and Bibles distributed.

In contextualization, positivist semiotics assumes that signs in other cultures, such as drama, drums, and music, are inherently tied to their pagan meanings and therefore cannot be used by Christians. This leads to widespread rejection of local signs, and the importation of Western Christian ones. We sing Western hymns translated into the local language, build churches in European styles, and import our liturgies. If we are Anglicans, we have priests; if Presbyterians, we have presbyters; if Baptists, we introduce voting. The result is a minimally contextualized approach to missions.

View Two: Uncritical Contextualization

The more deeply we are involved in cross-cultural ministries, the more we realize the reality of social, cultural, and historical contexts, the depth of the differences between them, and the difficulties in dealing with these differences. Early anthropologists and missionaries studied other cultures using Western theoretical frameworks. After the 1930s, anthropologists began to realize the importance of understanding the world as the people they study see it.[2] This led to a profound shift in the nature of anthropological and missiological theories, and to an on-going exploration of the differences between cultures and their mutual intelligibility. Can we truly understand others? Can we compare their cultures with our own and, if so, on what basis? We begin by study-ing the people we serve, but end with studying ourselves and our own assumptions. This process relativizes viewpoints and places them on equal footing (fig. 1.4).

Figure 1.4
View Two: *Uncritical Contextualization*

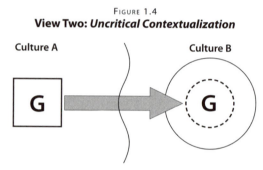

The growing awareness of anthropological insight into human contexts has led in missions to a growing awareness of the importance of radically contextualizing the gospel in other cultures to make it comprehensible and to allow people to become followers of Jesus Christ more easily. This awareness is the result of two paradigm shifts. The first was the emergence of Saussurian semiotics. Ferdinand de Saussure (1916) raised the question of the relationship between sign and reality, and came to the conclusion that it was arbitrary. In fact, he argued that signs do not refer to external realities at all, as formerly thought. Rather, they are mental constructs that create meaning systems in the mind. Signs have forms and meanings, but both are in the mind, and there are no links between signs and realities other than the conventionalities of human cultures. Meanings are wholly subjective (fig. 1.5). If this is true, then an accurate literal translation from one culture to another does not guarantee the preservation of the mean-

---

2. Bronislaw Malinowski and British structural anthropology pioneered ethnographic field-work that stressed living with people and learning to see the world the way they see it. This raised the question of whose perspectives are "right" and, eventually, to the belief in cultural relativism.

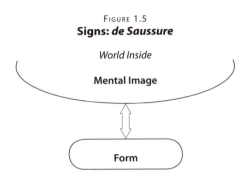

FIGURE 1.5
Signs: *de Saussure*

ing. Furthermore, we must measure communication not by what is said by the speaker but what is understood by the listener. We need translations in which mental meanings are preserved in cross-cultural communication rather than literal references. The result is dynamic equivalence, or receptor-oriented Bible translations.

The second paradigm shift occurred in epistemology. Positivism, which was the foundation for the Enlightenment, was increasingly challenged as false, arrogant, oppressive, and colonial. In its place emerged postmodern instrumentalism (also known as pragmatism), which sees knowledge systems as the creation of human minds. They are cultural Rorschachs, not photographs, of reality. There is no way to test whether they are true, so we adopt those that are most useful to us (Hiebert 1999; Laudan 1996). The result is cultural relativism. All cultures are considered to be equally good and true. None can judge another. Moreover, the preservation of cultures becomes an unquestioned good.

The introduction of Saussurian semiotics and instrumental epistemology profoundly challenged the fundamental assumptions of the Western mission movement and its colonial attitudes. Western "civilization" was no longer seen as superior and local cultures were to be valued. If there was good in all religions, why should missionaries seek to convert others at all? In any case, if missionaries do go, they should become insiders and identify fully with the people they serve. Local people should be encouraged to read the Scriptures for themselves and to formulate their own theologies.

The further outcome of the movement to contextualize occurred when culturally sensitive missionaries, such as E. S. Jones and Lesslie Newbigin, returned to their home countries. They began to look at these as mission fields and were shocked at the uncritical contextualization of the gospel in Western contexts (fig. 1.6). The gospel had become part of the culture, not an outside counter-culture community. It had largely lost its prophetic

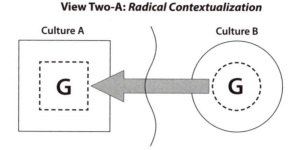

FIGURE 1.6
View Two-A: *Radical Contextualization*

voice. Furthermore, the culture itself had moved on, leaving the church behind. Out of their prophetic calls emerged the Gospel in Our Culture movement.[3] This movement has combined strong critique of the Western churches for having become outdated with a call for the radical contextualization of the gospel in North America by becoming seeker sensitive.

View Three: Critical Contextualization

In recent years there has been a reaction to radical contextualization. The questions arise: Is the gospel still the gospel when it is radically contextualized, or has it become captive to the cultural context? Does the most contextualized gospel lead to the most vital, biblical churches? Out of this concern has emerged a critical approach to contextualization (fig. 1.7). Central to critical contextualization is the fact that the gospel cannot be equated with any contextual expression of it. As Andrew Walls notes:

> No one ever meets universal Christianity in itself: we only ever meet Christianity in a local form and that means a historically, culturally conditioned form. We need not fear this; when God became man he became historically, culturally conditioned man in a particular time and place. What he became, we need not fear to be. There is nothing wrong in having local forms of Christianity—provided that we remember that they are local. (1996, 235)

Contextualization is an important and valuable process, necessary to the communication of the gospel. But culturally, contextualized Christianity is always a reflection of a much deeper universal reality.

---

3. It is important to note that both Jones and Newbigin, in their encounters with Hinduism, moved well beyond an instrumentalist view and religious relativism to affirming the truth of the gospel and the need to bear bold witness to it. In North America, the Gospel in Our Culture movement is led by George Hunsberger and Craig Van Gelder (1996), inspired by the writings of Lesslie Newbigin (1986; 1989).

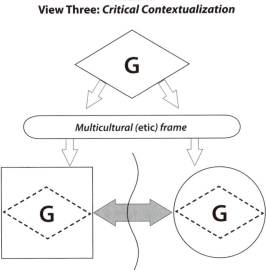

FIGURE 1.7
View Three: *Critical Contextualization*

Underlying this new paradigm is a rejection of Saussurian semiotics and the emergence of Peircian semiotics (fig. 1.8). Charles Peirce, an American mathematician and linguist, proposed a third way of looking at signs. He rejected the dualism of form and meaning introduced by Humboldt and Saussure and introduced instead a triadic view of signs. Each sign, he said, had (1) the sign (the signifier; e.g., the spoken or written word, the sound of a bell, a picture of an arrow); (2) the mental concept or image it evokes in the mind (the signified); and (3) the reality to which it refers (the significatum). For example, the word *tree* points to real trees in the forest and invokes a mental image of a tree at the same time. In other words, a sign is the

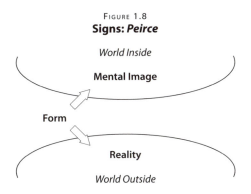

FIGURE 1.8
Signs: *Peirce*

linking of mental images to realities by means of words, gestures, sounds, and images. They have an objective dimension and a subjective dimension. This means that they are not simply arbitrary human constructs. However humans conceive of their worlds—and they do so in many different ways— their cultures must reflect in fundamental ways the order of reality itself. If there were not a great deal of correspondence between a peoples' view of reality and reality itself, life would be impossible. Driving down a road, we would need to watch out not only for mentally constructed traffic but also for traffic that is indeed real and deadly.

There is also a growing reaction to postmodern instrumentalism and the emergence of a post-postmodern critical realist epistemology (Hiebert 1999; Laudan 1977).[4] According to this view, humans can know reality in part. But their knowledge is not a photograph of reality with a one-to-one correspondence between theory and facts. It is more like a map. Maps must correspond to reality in what they claim to affirm, but they are mental images that are schematic, approximate, and—of necessity—limited and selective. A road map does not make truth claims about property boundaries or economic variables. Moreover, to be useful it must be simple, not showing every bend in the road or every pothole or bridge. However, it must get drivers to their intended destinations.

Given Peircian semiotics and a critical realist epistemology, it is possible to compare human belief systems and to test them against reality. To do so, we need to develop metacultural grids that enable us to evaluate different worldviews, to translate between them, and to negotiate between them.[5] In Bible translation, Peircian semiotics leads beyond dynamic equivalence to double translations in which the translators seek to communicate ideas accurately while preserving as much as possible the historical realities spoken of in Scripture, often by using footnotes or parenthetical clarifications.

4. Charles Sanders Peirce wrote in the late nineteenth century. He named his epistemological theory "pragmatism." William James and John Dewey drew on his insights but transformed the theory so fundamentally that in the end Peirce rejected it and renamed his theory "pragmaticism." This term never caught on, and many believe that Peirce is the father of what currently is known as pragmatism or instrumentalism and of epistemological relativism. Peirce's epistemology was not relativistic, but it was the basis for what is now known as critical realism.

5. There is no one true metacultural grid. Rather, metacultural frames are created by people from different cultures gathering together and comparing the way they translate between cultures, something all transcultural people learn to do, even if they give little thought to it. Developing suitable metacultural and metatheological frames is the first step in building mutual understanding among people from different contexts, and for comparing and evaluating these contexts in the light of divine revelation.

The new view calls for critical contextualization or practicing missional theology (Hiebert and Tiénou 2006). The Bible is seen as containing divine revelation, not simply humanly constructed beliefs. In contextualization, the heart of the gospel must be kept by encoding it in forms that are understood by the people, without making the gospel captive to the contexts. This is an ongoing process of embodying the gospel in an ever-changing world. Here cultures are viewed as both good and evil, not simply as neutral vehicles for understanding the world. No culture is absolute or privileged. We are all relativized by the gospel.

A critical realist epistemology differentiates between revelation and theology. The former is God-given truth; the latter is human understandings of that truth and cannot be equated fully with it. Human knowledge is always partial and schematic, and does not correspond one-to-one with reality. Our theology is our understanding of Scripture in our contexts. It may be true, but it is always partial and perspectival. It seeks to answer the questions we raise. This calls for a community-based hermeneutics in which dialogue serves to correct the biases of individuals. On the global scale, this calls for both local and global theologies. Local churches have the right to interpret and apply the gospel in their contexts, but also a responsibility to join the larger church community around the world in seeking to overcome the limited perspectives each brings, and the biases each has that might distort the gospel.

In this view of contextualization, missionaries are transcultural people—outsiders and insiders at the same time, people who come to serve the local churches as fellow believers and mediators, not as inside rivals for power and position (as we will see in chapters 8 and 9).

Views of Scripture

While affirming that Scripture is divine revelation, it is important to keep in mind that the Scriptures themselves were given to humans in particular historical and sociocultural contexts (fig. 1.9). This is obvious to Old and New Testament scholars but is often overlooked by ordinary Christians. Differentiating between eternal truth and the particular contexts in the Bible is not an easy task, but is essential if we are to understand the heart of the gospel, which is for everyone.

Nonetheless, a full view of the gospel in human contexts must emphasize that the gospel is indeed divine revelation to humans, not humans searching for the truth (fig. 1.10). This revelation is given in the particularities of history and locality. But it is given by God and reveals God's universal message to all humankind. It is easy, particularly in the academy, to ask what humans think about God. We must always remember, as Charles Malik reminds us (1987), that the real question is: what does God think about us? It is difficult in a pluralist world to affirm with deep love that the gospel is uniquely God speaking to us, not just human theological reflections about

FIGURE 1.9
Scripture Given in Human Contexts

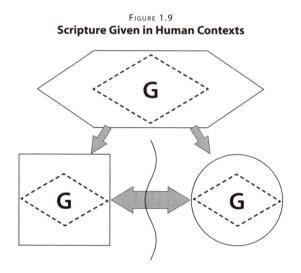

FIGURE 1.10
God's Revelation to Humans

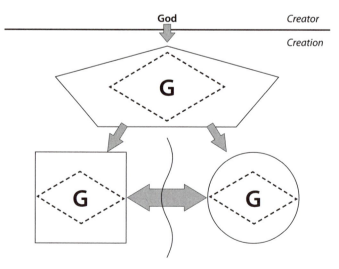

ultimate realities. But, as E. Stanley Jones points out (1925), we are called not to be God's lawyers, but to bear bold *witness* to the truth that Jesus Christ is the only way to God and his kingdom. If we truly believe this is true, then to affirm other ways is to withhold from people knowledge of the way to eternal salvation.

Gospel and Human Contexts

What, then, is the relationship between gospel and human contexts, and how can we communicate the gospel to people in their contexts? Three principles can help us here.

The first principle is that the gospel must not be equated with any particular human context, not even the biblical cultural context: gospel *versus* cultures. Not only is this true with regard to Western Christianity, but it is also true with respect to the Scriptures. The gospel was revealed in the historical and sociocultural contexts of the Old and New Testaments, but those contexts are not normative for Christianity around the world.

It is important to remember that the gospel is distinct from human cultures, but this does not set the two in opposition to each other. Rather the two are separate, interrelated realities. We must recognize that divine revelation was given to humans in particular social and cultural contexts, and so the gospel is not to be equated with any one of these contexts.

The second principle we need to keep in mind is that the gospel must be put in specific sociocultural contexts for people to understand it: gospel *in* cultures. To do so we must seek to understand and study both the Scriptures and human cultures, and to incarnate the gospel in these cultures without losing its distinct divine nature.

The third principle to guide us in understanding the relationship of the gospel to human social and cultural contexts is that the gospel is transformative—gospel *transforming* culture. The gospel is not simply a message to be affirmed as true, but a call to follow Christ throughout life in radical discipleship. Newbigin (1989) speaks of the relationship of church to culture in terms of a missionary "encounter" with culture.

In transformation, we must begin where people are and help them grow, just as God begins with us where we are but leads us into maturity and faithfulness. Conversion is to turn to follow Christ, as individuals and as churches (Hiebert 1982). It is the first step in spiritual growth and obedience. This transformation must be both personal and corporate. As individuals we need to be *born again* into a new life. As a church we need to model not the ways of this world, but the ways of the Kingdom, and to challenge the evils in our societies and cultures.

In transformation, we need to involve people in evaluating their own cultures in the light of new truth. This draws on their strength. They know their old culture better than we do and are in a better position to critique it and live transformed lives within it, once they have biblical instruction. We can bring outside views that help them see their own cultural biases, but they are the ones who make decisions as they grow spiritually through learning discernment and applying scriptural teachings to their own lives. The gospel is not simply information to be communicated. It is a message to which people must respond. Moreover, it is not enough that leaders be convinced that changes are needed. They may share their convictions and point out the consequences of various decisions, but they and their people must together make and enforce the decisions they have arrived at corporately. Only then will old beliefs and practices not be pushed underground, subverting the gospel.

In transformation, we must deal with the deeper issues involved. Too often we act on immediate cases at hand and do not use them to stimulate longer-range reflection on the underlying issues. Specific cases should stimulate further reflection in systematic and biblical theologies and human studies that facilitate well-grounded responses to the personal, social, and cultural contexts at hand.

Transformational theology focuses on mission. It takes humans seriously in the particularity of their persons, societies, and cultures, and their ever-changing histories. It integrates cognition, affectivity, and evaluation in its response to biblical truth and defines faith not simply as mental affirmations of truth, or as positive experiences of God, but as beliefs, feelings, and morals that lead to obedience to the word of God. It rejects the division between pure and applied theology, and sees ministry both as a way of doing theology and as a form of worship.

Missiology as a Discipline

Missiology is an academic discipline like systematic theology, anthropology, and history. A discipline or research tradition is defined not by the theories it generates as answers, but by the central questions it asks, the data it examines, and the methods it legitimates.

The central question of missiology is: how can the gospel of Jesus Christ be incarnated in human contexts so that people understand and believe, societies are transformed, and the kingdom of God is made manifest on earth as it is in heaven? Behind this question is the greater question: what is God's mission in creating and redeeming the world? Missiology's central question can be broken down into many subquestions, such as: (1) What is the relationship of human missions to God's mission? (2) What is the nature of the gospel in a particular human context? (3) How can the gospel be communicated so that people believe? and (4) How does the gospel transform societies?

Missiology seeks to integrate four bodies of data into a single discipline: theology, anthropology, Scripture, and church history. Each of these bodies is the basis for another discipline. In this sense, missiology is an integrative discipline drawing on four sets of theories and findings to answer its central question.

The four bodies of data can be diagrammed on two axes, the axis between divine revelation and human contexts, and the axis between synchronic and diachronic analysis (fig. 1.11). Along the vertical axis, missiology must understand the gospel in order to communicate it to humans in the particularities of their lives. Here missiology draws on systematic and biblical theologies. Missiology also studies humans. Here it draws on the social sciences, humanities, and history to understand people. Just as systematic and biblical theologians need to guard against becoming captive to the human rational and historical methods of the academy, so, too, missiologists must understand the theories they draw from the social sciences and humanities, lest they become captive to worldviews that subvert the gospel.

Figure 1.11
Missiology as a Discipline

Along the horizontal axis, studies can be either synchronic or diachronic. Synchronic studies examine the basic structures of reality as they exist at a single point in time. For example, synchronic studies of Scripture lead to systematic theology. Synchronic studies in the sciences lead to biological, psychological, social, cultural, and spiritual models of human beings that identify the different elements of the human makeup and demonstrate the relationships among those elements. For instance, a doctor may study various systems, such as the nervous, skeletal, muscular, and digestive systems, and the relationships among these. Synchronic theories seek to formulate broad generalizations from large bodies of data and to enable us to control our lives in certain ways.

Diachronic studies look at the underlying story of the data being examined. In the case of individuals, this is their biographies; in the case of humans, it is their history. In missions this includes the study of the history of God's mission in the Old and New Testaments and the history of the church since then. Here the models identify starting points, plot, and ending points to demonstrate meaning in the data that otherwise would be a disconnected set of historical happenings. Diachronic theories seek to formulate an understanding of divine and human purposes in history.

FIGURE 1.12
Missiology and Related Disciplines

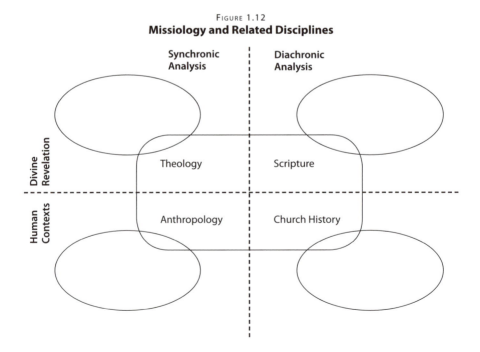

The central question of missiology is: how can the gospel be incarnated? This question is addressed in a unified way by drawing on data from the study of both divine revelation and human contexts, each conducted in both synchronic and diachronic fashion. Theology, anthropology, the study of Scripture, and church history all contribute.

Missiology and Other Disciplines

It is clear that missiology must draw on and contribute to a number of related fields: systematic theology, biblical theology, social sciences, and history (fig. 1.12). The relationships with these have been varied. With the rise of the university, disciplines have carved out and laid claim to their own territories. The academy is no longer a *uni*-versity but a *multi*-versity. The result is reductionist or stratigraphic worldviews that disintegrate reality into many parts, losing the picture of the whole. What is needed is community hermeneutics involving scholars in related disciplines, learning and sharing with those in missiology who specialize in cognate fields: historians and mission historians, systematic theologians and mission theologians, and social science disciplines with missiologists specializing in these fields.

Missiologists representing the different fields, through community hermeneutics, must work to integrate their subfields into one unified discipline with one vision. This will require revising the theories in each of the subdisciplines to make them complementary to one another, not contradictory. On a higher level it requires metatheories that bridge the gap between different fields of missiology and enable us to grasp, if only "as in a mirror darkly," the big picture and big story of God and his mission. These metatheories need to show the relationship between divine revelation and human contexts, and between diachronic and synchronic theories of reality. The next chapter provides a model for how this can be done.

2

Missional Theology

TITE TIÉNOU AND PAUL G. HIEBERT

In recent years, missiologists have increasingly drawn on the insights the human sciences provide for their work. One key question keeps arising: how can missions keep from becoming captive to the sciences, and how can the findings of the sciences be integrated into missions while retaining solid theological foundations? This problem of relating theology to science is not unique to missions. It underlies much of the discussion about the inclusion of psychology in training ministers and Christian counselors, the integration of medical sciences and Christian healing, and the use of modern business sciences in the administration of churches and church institutions. Despite these discussions, a big chasm often exists between theology and the sciences.

At a deep level, the problem of integrating theology and the sciences is a worldview issue. It is due, in part, to our definitions and perceptions of what constitutes theology and what constitutes science. We now examine these two critical bodies of knowledge and suggest avenues for a rapprochement between them.

This chapter first appeared in *Missiology: An International Review* 34, no. 2 (April 2006): 219–38. Tite Tiénou is dean and professor of theology of missions at Trinity Evangelical Divinity School in Deerfield, Illinois. He is the author of numerous scholarly articles and *The Theological Task of the Church in Africa*, 2nd ed. (Achimota, Ghana: Africa Christian Press, 1990).

Research Traditions

Larry Laudan (1977) classifies the sciences as "research traditions"—bodies of knowledge shared by communities of scholars seeking to understand the truth in their fields. Each research tradition is determined by: (1) the critical questions it seeks to answer, (2) the body of data it examines, and (3) the methods it accepts as valid means for discovering answers (fig. 2.1). Each is embedded in a worldview—the fundamental assumptions it makes about reality. Different answers or theories are offered in response to key questions, and competing ones are debated until one or the other emerges as accepted doctrine, until it is further questioned.

For example, as a research tradition physics is the study of the building blocks of the material world, which it assumes are real. It examines material objects using experiments, electron microscopes, ion chambers, and other means to find answers to questions such as: What are the basic components of matter? What are the major physical forces? And how do these interact?

FIGURE 2.1
Levels of Cultural Knowledge

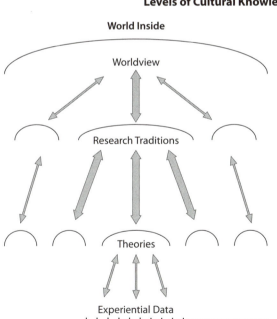

World Inside

Worldview

- provides ontological, affective, and normative assumptions on which the culture builds its world
- integrates belief systems into a single worldview

Research Traditions

- determine domain of examination
- define questions to be asked
- provide methods for investigation
- integrate theories in belief systems and worldview
- mediate between empirical realities

Theories

- answer questions raised by belief systems
- order experience into theories

Experiential Data

World Outside

Theology, too, is a research tradition. It is a body of knowledge debated by a community of scholars seeking to answer certain critical questions. On the level of theories, there are debates over Calvinism and Arminianism; premillennial, postmillennial, and amillennial eschatologies; and orthodoxy, liberalism, and neo-orthodoxy. These are true arguments because the different proponents are seeking to answer the same questions using accepted methods. In other words, theology is a research tradition not because it has arrived at one universally agreed upon answer, but because those in the field are seeking to answer the same questions by using accepted methods of inquiry in their examination of the same data.

Ways of Doing Theology

If theology is a research tradition, how does this change our perception of it as a discipline, and how does it change its relationship to the sciences? Before responding to these questions, we need to clarify what we mean by theology. We are assuming here that Scripture is divine revelation given to us by God, not our human search for God. Theology, then, is our attempt to understand that revelation in our historical and cultural contexts (fig. 2.2). As Millard Erickson notes, it is a second-level activity (1998). It is important, therefore, that we study Scripture carefully so that our theologies are biblically informed.

We must remember, however, that all our theologies are shaped by our societies and cultures. We must also remember that there are great gulfs between biblical times and our times, between universal theories and the particulars of everyday life, and between synchronic theologies that examine the unchanging structure of reality and diachronic theologies that

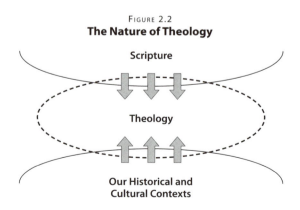

FIGURE 2.2
The Nature of Theology

Scripture

Theology

**Our Historical and
Cultural Contexts**

study cosmic history. It is important in any theological reflection to work toward bridging these differences.

Theology, like the sciences, is divided into different research traditions, each one seeking to answer specific questions by making particular assumptions and using different methods of research (fig. 2.3). Here we briefly examine two of these types, philosophical/systematic theology and biblical theology—and suggest a third way of doing theology that complements the other two.[1]

Philosophical and Systematic Theology

One approach to the study of Scripture is to use the assumptions, questions, and methods of philosophy. This led to systematic theology, which emerged in the twelfth century with the reintroduction of Greek logic from the universities of the Middle East and Spain (Finger 1985, 21–28).[2] At first, systematic theology was viewed as the "queen of the sciences," but over time it became only one discipline among others in theological education—alongside biblical exegesis, hermeneutics, history, missions, and other disciplines.

The central question that systematic theology seeks to answer is: what are the unchanging universals of reality? It assumes that there are basic, unchanging realities, and if these are known we can understand the fundamental structure of all reality.[3] It also assumes that ultimate truth can be known by means of human reason, and that this truth is ahistorical and acultural—it is true for everyone everywhere. Philosophical theology uses the abstract, algorithmic logic, digital categories of Greek philosophy, which are propositional in nature. It rejects all internal contradictions and

1. We will not examine the doxological or tropological theology of Eastern Orthodoxy, which is done in the context of worship and stresses the mystical, sacramental, and iconic nature of truth. The key question addressed is: how can we comprehend complex, transcendent truths about God and reality that lie beyond words, logic, and human reason? Orthodox theology uses nondiscursive signs and tropes such as icons, metaphors, types, and parables to communicate transcendent truth. For an analysis of doxological theology see Wainwright (1980); for tropological or metaphorical theology see McFague (1982).

2. Systematic theology is based on the resurgence of Platonic realism that gave rise to Scholasticism and later the humanistic school of Erasmus, culminating in the Enlightenment school. For a historical summary of its emergence, see Fuller (1997); see also McGrath (1998).

3. This thought is rooted in the Newtonian assumption that everything is composed of basic building blocks put together as a machine. This view leads to determinism and an engineering approach to reality based on technological solutions. It also leads to the division of the sciences into disconnected disciplines, which creates a division of labor and a gap between experts and laity.

FIGURE 2.3
Types of Theology

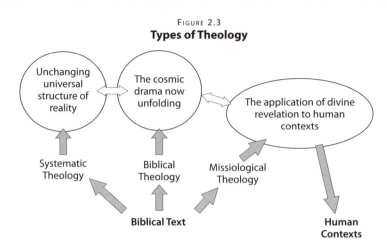

fuzziness in categories and thought.[4] Its goal is to construct a single systematic understanding of ultimate truth that is comprehensive, logically consistent, and conceptually coherent.[5] To arrive at objective truth, it, like the modern sciences, separates cognition from feelings and values, because the latter are thought to introduce subjectivity into the process.

The strength of systematic theology is its examination of the fundamental elements and categories in Scripture. It gives us a standard to test our knowledge and helps us to understand in some measure the biblical worldview—the view of reality as God sees it and as he has revealed it to us in Scripture.

Systematic theology has its limitations. Because, like Greek thought, it focuses on a synchronic analysis of the ultimate, unchanging structure of reality, it loses sight of the cosmic drama or plot in the Scriptures and the role history and historical events play in that drama. It cannot adequately deal with change, and must see changes in God's attitudes and responses as surface phenomena, not intrinsic to God's ultimate nature.[6]

4. An algorithm is a formal logical process that, if carried out correctly, produces the right answer. Algorithmic logic is sometimes called "machine" logic because it is the basis on which calculators and computers work, and can be done faster and more accurately by these than by humans. For an introduction to fuzzy categories and fuzzy logic, see Hiebert 1994, 107–36.

5. Peter Lombard founded systematic theology when he sought to disengage key theological questions from their original biblical contexts and to arrange them in a logical sequence of their own that would provide a comprehensive, coherent, and synthetically consistent account of all the major issues of Christian faith, and demonstrate the rational credibility of Christian faith (Finger 1985, 19). Lombard's *Sentences*, written in the 1140s, provided the form for much of later medieval and Reformation theology (McGrath 1998).

6. Unlike Newton, who looked for systems that change over time, Einstein, in his theory of general relativity, argues that space and time are not absolute grids within which nature exists but are part of that existence itself (Bodanis 2000). Moreover, time is not a separate variable

Because systematic theology focuses on universals and an ascent to knowledge through contemplation divorced from everyday life, it does not tell us how to deal with the beliefs and practices found in different cultures or times, or with the particularities of our own lives. Its focus on abstraction and rational coherence has often turned it into an intellectual exercise remote from life's everyday issues. Moreover, the Greek distinction between *pure* and *applied* knowledge has relegated the problems of everyday life to a position of lesser importance, since they deal with the subjective, changing messiness of human lives.

Philosophical theology is also in danger of becoming captive to the methods of philosophy.[7] In the West, the search for a comprehensive system based on digital sets and algorithmic logic implies that humans can grasp the fullness of truth with clarity. It leaves little room for the particularities and ambiguities of life, the mysteries that transcend human comprehension, and the wisdom that can deal with the contradictions and paradoxes of a rapidly changing world (Yancey 2000).

Systematic theology too often has a weak sense of mission. Thomas Finger notes, "Systematic theology arose as a branch of academic study pursued in universities and not primarily as a task of the church involved in the world at large" (1985, 20–21). Missiology is not a category in systematic theology, and systematic theology is not the driving force behind missions.[8] Missiology is commonly relegated to the category of practical theology.

---

apart from the three dimensions of space. It is the fourth dimension. We cannot start with a static view of reality and then introduce time and change. To leave time out of our analysis is like trying to describe a three-dimensional world in two-dimensional terms. Consequently, to speak of unchanging, timeless universals in creation is to omit an essential dimension of creation itself. One consequence of this is that when God, the Creator, reveals himself to humans in his creation, he does so not only in space but also in time. At the heart of creation and the gospel is God's Story.

7. For discussions about doing theology from non-Western perspectives, see Taber (1978), Schneider (1985), Schultz (1989), Lee (1978), and Tiénou (1990; 1993). One issue philosophical theology must wrestle with is the fact that different cultures use different logics—each of which is perfectly logical and internally consistent, but differs from the others in the assumptions it makes. For example, much of modern logic is based on digital sets: all things can be sorted into different discrete, nonoverlapping categories. In numbers theory, this sees numbers as intervals. This is true of Euclidian geometry and Cantonan algebra. Other logics, such as Indian logic and calculus, see numbers as ratios—as infinite continua from one point to another (Zadeh 1965). Greek logic is abstract and analytical. Other logics are concrete, function (Luria 1976), and narrative (Fisher 1987). Can we do philosophical theology using different logics and, if so, what are the strengths and weaknesses of each of these logics?

8. On the one hand, few trained as theologians go into missions, and many schools with strong departments of theology have no department or vision of missions. On the other hand, all missionaries, of necessity, must become theologians.

Finally, systematic theology was itself a product and reflection of Western intellectual history. Calvin, Luther, and their successors appealed not only to *sola Scriptura* but to logic, rhetoric, and other methods available to them to shape their theologies. In so doing, they allowed scholasticism in the back door. Gerhard Ebling notes,

> What was the relation of the systematic method here [in the post-Reformation] to the exegetical method? Ultimately it was the same as in the medieval scholasticism. There, too, exegesis of holy scripture went on not only within systematic theology, but also separately alongside of it, yet so that the possibility of a tension between exegesis and systematic theology was *a priori* excluded. Exegesis was enclosed within the frontiers fixed by systematic theology. (1963, 82–83)

Systematic theologians need to examine the cultural and historical contexts in which they formulate their theologies to discern the biases that these might introduce in their understanding of Scripture. All theologies are human creations seeking to understand divine revelation, and all theologies are embedded in histories and worldviews that shape the way they see things. There are no culture-free and history-free theologies. We all read Scripture from the perspectives of our particular context. This does not mean we can know no truth. It does mean that we must never equate our theology with Scripture, and that we need to work in hermeneutical communities and draw on those who have gone before us to check our personal and cultural biases.

Philosophical theologies are now being done by committed evangelical theologians around the world. But different human contexts raise different questions that require theological reflection. Donald Schultz writes: "The time is also past when Western theologians had all the 'definitive answers.' Asian theologians now bear the responsibility and willingly accept it. The latter have discovered that Western definitive answers do not automatically fit the Asian situation and often answer questions not asked in Asia" (1989, 23).

Biblical Theology

A second theological research tradition that emerged in the West was biblical theology. Reacting to the scholasticism of post-Reformation theologians, Johann Gabler advocated a new way of doing theology. He saw theology as a practical science and stressed experience and the illumination of the Spirit. Gabler's central question was: what did the biblical passages mean at the time of those who wrote them, and what lessons for today can we learn from them? In asking this he advocated a return to the Bible as history, with an emphasis on the unfolding of the cosmic story.

Biblical theology examines the narrative nature of Scripture. It assumes that the heart of revelation is historical in character: there is a real world with a real history of change over time that is "going somewhere" and that has meaning because it has a plot that culminates in God's eternal reign.[9] Biblical theology argues that this view of truth as cosmic story is fundamental to the Hebrew worldview and to an understanding of Scripture. To describe ultimate reality, the Jews told and reenacted in rituals the acts of God in their lives. As Wolfhart Pannenberg reminds us, God is not only the ground of all existence, but all of history is a revelation of his existence and reign (1968).

Biblical theology uses the questions, methods, and assumptions of modern historiography.[10] It uses the temporal logic of antecedent and consequent causality, and accepts teleological explanations in which God and humans act on the basis of intentions. Biblical theology is important because it gives us the diachronic dimension of a biblical worldview. It gives meaning to life by helping us see the cosmic story in which human history and our biographies are embedded.

Biblical theology also has its limits. It focuses on diachronic meaning, leaving the unchanging synchronic structure of reality in our peripheral vision. It focuses on past biblical history, not on present events. It looks at the universal story, not the particular lives of individuals and communities outside the biblical narrative. It does not directly help us apply biblical truth to the problems we face in specific cultures and persons today. If we are not careful, it can become a study unto itself with little relevance to us today. We must focus on the cosmic story, but we need to remember that God speaks to us through Scripture in the context of concrete settings of human and personal history, and that our stories as individuals and as the church are part of that cosmic story.

9. I use the term plot here in the way that Paul speaks of the "mystery" now revealed to us (Rom. 16:25; Eph. 1:9; 3:3; 6:19; Col. 1:26). This is to say that there is real history, that it is moving in a direction and not changing randomly, and that behind it there is a plot or drama—a cosmic story—that gives it meaning because it is "going somewhere." For us it is the story of God creating a perfect world, redeeming the lost who turn in faith to him, and restoring creation to perfection in which all will bow before Christ the Lord.

10. For G. Vos, biblical theology is the "history of special revelation" (1948, 23). Biblical theology is historical; systematic theology is logical.

Biblical theology is essential to our understanding of Scripture, but like systematic theology, God's mission in the world, particularly as that relates to us today, is not a central theme in its analysis. It has not been a strong motivating force driving people and churches into missions.

Missional Theology

To communicate the gospel in human contexts, we need a third way of doing theology—a way of thinking biblically about God's universal mission in the context of the world here and now, with all its particularities, paradoxes, and confusions. We refer to this third theology as *missional theology*, although the same principles of studying Scripture, studying humans, and incarnating the gospel in human life apply equally to pastors, church elders, and indeed to every Christian.[11]

Missionaries, by the very nature of their task, must become theologians. Almost a century ago Martin Kähler wrote, "Mission is the mother of theology." Theology began as an accompanying manifestation of Christian missions, and not as a luxury of the world-dominating church. David Bosch notes, "Paul was the first Christian theologian precisely because he was the first Christian missionary" (1991, 124). Elwood points out that "Asian theology cannot afford to be purely academic and philosophical, but rather it is valid only if it is produced not primarily in between piles of books, but in the 'field' where it is put to the test every day" (1980, 75).

The questions arise: how do mission theologians do theology, and how is this different from other ways of doing theology? Their central question is: what is God's Word to humans in their particular situations? Mission theologians assume that God is a missionary God, that mission is the central theme in God's acts on earth, and that all Christians are to be a part of this mission. They also assume that all humans live in different historical and sociocultural settings, and that the gospel must be made known to them in the particularity of these contexts. Eugene Peterson writes,

> This is the gospel focus: *you* are the man; *you* are the woman. The gospel is never about everybody else; it is always about you, about me. The gospel is never truth in general; it's always a truth in specific. The gospel is never

11. The need to contextualize the gospel in human cultures became obvious as missionaries went to other societies. As long as people live and minister within their own culture, they are largely unaware of their own culture and worldview, and how these shape their understandings of the gospel. Missionaries, however, confront deep cultural differences immediately—culture shock—starting with differences in language, culture, theology, and worldview.

a commentary on ideas or culture or conditions; it's always about actual persons, actual pains, actual troubles, actual sin; you, me; who you are and what you've done; who I am and what I've done. (1997, 185)

The task of the mission theologian is to translate and communicate the gospel in the language and culture of real people in the particularities of their lives so that it may transform them, their societies, and their cultures into what God intends for them to be. Missional theology seeks to build the bridge between biblical revelation and human contexts. It seeks to remove the gap between orthodoxy and orthopraxy,[12] between truth, love, and holiness.

One systematic logic and methodology that missional theology can use by way of analogy is that of American law.[13] In the United States there are three levels of law: constitutional law, statutory law, and case law (fig. 2.4; see Romantz and Vinson, 1998). The Constitution is the unchanging foundation on which the legal system is built. Constitutional law exam-

12. Western theology is deeply influenced by the Platonic dualism of supernatural/natural, spirit/matter, mind/body, evangelism/social ministry, religion/science, faith/fact, and miracle/natural. The biblical view is contingent dualism: Creator/creation, God/humans (in the incarnation), eternal/temporal. This is dualism, but it is contingent in that God is eternal and the source of all creation, and creation is constantly dependent on God's ongoing creation for its very existence every moment it exists. In biblical thought the incarnation of God is far more profound than in Greek thought, where an invisible god in the heavens involves himself in a material world.

13. The use of law as a model is based on how legal systems seek to interpret corporate or universal principles in specific human situations. Like all human models, including those of philosophy and history, the method has its limitations and weaknesses. Different cultures handle the legal problems of everyday life differently. Indian villages use *panchayats*, or councils of elders. *Palavers* are found in West Africa. All these seek to apply moral principles to specific situations using different logics that are embedded in the broader method of wisdom. The relevance of these methods for doing missional theology needs to be studied. Most of them lack a set of eternal absolutes that determine ultimate truth and morality. These are determined by social consensus, not divine revelation that shows us truth and morality as God sees and has revealed them to us. The result is situational truth and morality.

Christian theologians in non-Western countries have sought to bridge the gap between theology and concrete human situations. Latin American theologians insist that we cannot separate orthodoxy from orthopraxy, which is an important corrective. To bridge the two they set up processes for the doing of theology, but do not provide systematic methods for exegeting Scripture or humans and for bridging the gulf between them. African theologians rightly insist that we must understand God in terms of his relationship with us, but to do so we must know who he is, and who we are in our common humanity and our personal, social, and cultural diversity. We use the American legal system here as an analogy not because it is the only or privileged way of doing missional theology, but because it has a fully developed methodology, which is a requirement for any research tradition that has an absolute reference point that avoids relativism and captivity to human contexts, and because it builds on a deep and careful study of the absolutes and the particularities of human life and builds a bridge between them.

ines statutory and case laws to see if any violate the Constitution. If they do, they are declared invalid. Statutory laws are laws passed by legitimate government bodies such as Congress, state governments, and government agencies. They seek to interpret constitutional principles in a changing world. For example, the introduction of new technologies and information has necessitated that federal agencies determine what is private property. Case laws are the legal guidelines that emerge out of legal rulings in precedent cases on specific instances. Judges are bound by the principle of *stare decisis*, which calls for them to make their judgments in accordance with the legal findings by judges in the past on similar cases, except where such precedents can be shown to be misinterpretations of the Constitution or legal statutes. In other words, judges must take into account the community of law around them, including decisions by judges who have gone before. Their findings contribute to a growing, dynamic body of case law that applies general principles to specific cases.

Figure 2.4
Modern Legal System

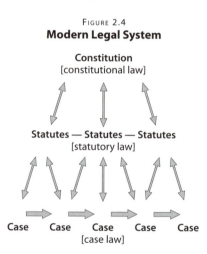

In missional theology, systematic theology plays the role of constitutional law. It helps us to understand the ultimate realities with which all reflections regarding human contexts and specific human cases must take account. It is important to remember that systematic theology is our understanding of unchanging universals based on our study of Scripture, and does not carry the authority of biblical revelation. Consequently, we must constantly test it against Scripture as we deal with the realities of life.

Biblical theology, church creeds, and confessions play the role of statutory law. They show how the universal principles revealed in Scripture have been manifest in biblical history and interpreted by God's people down through history in an ever-changing world. Both systematic and biblical theology are the reflections of the church in its attempt to understand divine revelation.

Missional theology draws on systematic theology and biblical theology to understand the gospel. It also draws on precedent cases in the life of the church—on the way other Christians have reflected and ruled in similar situations. There are three essential steps in missional methodology (fig. 2.5).

FIGURE 2.5
Steps in Missional Methodology

Phenomenology
• study the situation as we see it
• seek to understand how the people see it
• develop a comparative frame to compare and evaluate different views

Ontology
• do "reality" checks on the facts
• study scriptural teachings on the case
• evaluate and make decisions on the case

Missiology
• act on the immediate case
• begin procedure to deal with the underlying issues in the long run

Phenomenology

The first step in missional methodology is phenomenology—a careful study of the specific case at hand—including the participants, the events, and the sociocultural and historical contexts. This is the crucial fact-finding stage, the "pain and anguish of giving birth to the facts which are compared with those in earlier cases" (Levi 1949, v). Most missionaries and ministers are well trained to study Scripture, but few have training in exegeting humans. Consequently, their message is misunderstood by the people they serve. An example illustrates the great cultural gaps we need to bridge. After teaching about the parable of the sower and the seed to local women, the missionary asked what lesson they could learn from the story. They laughed and said that that is what happens when you let men plant seed. They simply throw it everywhere on the ground. As women, they would never do that. They would carefully dig holes in good soil and plant a seed or two in each hole. For effective missions we need to understand humans as much as we understand the gospel.

In the examination of human realities, the human sciences—particularly anthropology because of its global view, its comparative approach, and its focus on the social and cultural contexts in which people live and the particularities of real human life—are of vital importance. We begin by studying the situation as we see it. We must then seek to understand the situation as the people involved see it. This involves studying local practices, rituals, beliefs, and worldviews, because these inform behavior. This analysis, however, does not provide us with a full understanding of a situation or a bridge for deciding on a biblical solution. We need to compare these different perspectives, ours and others, and develop a metacultural framework to compare and evaluate the different points of view (fig. 2.6). Because anthropology studies different social and cultural systems, it helps us to build bridges of understanding and evaluation between them.

Figure 2.6
Cross-Cultural Comparisons

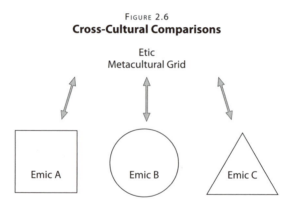

Ontology

The second step in missional methodology is to examine the phenomenological claims in light of reality checks and Scripture, and to judge the situation in light of reality as we understand it. We need systematic and biblical theologies to understand the structure and story underlying the biblical narratives. Here human studies can also help us understand divine revelation, which was always given in particular historical and sociocultural contexts.

We need also to examine how other Christians have dealt with similar situations. Case law is based on the process of reasoning by comparison with precedent cases. This requires the presentation of competing examples and the articulation of similarities and differences between them. Levi writes, "A working legal system must therefore be willing to pick out key similarities and to reason from them to the justice of applying a common classification" (1949, 3). In the process, classifications are created and refined as the relevant classification of the particular case is made. Moreover, the categories must be left ambiguous to some extent in order to permit their application to new and different cases, and to allow for growth in understanding the laws themselves. Laws are not rigid formulae mechanically and blindly applied to human situations. They are the reflections of people seeking to build a moral community.

Morality is not based on a set of impersonal laws that exist apart from God. These laws are God's moral commands, and righteousness is living in right relationship with God, with one another, and with the world. Missional theology is God's people seeking to live as God's people in a fallen and ever-changing world, and to bear witness to God's kingdom to the world around them. As in the case of legal reflection, it is important in our theological reflections to realize that the mechanism of theological reasoning should not be obscured by the illusion that theology is a system of known rules that simply need to be applied in a specific case. Levi notes that too often we have seen the legal process as though it were "a method of applying general rules of law to diverse facts—in short, as though the doctrine of precedent meant that general rules, once properly determined, remained unchanging, and then were applied, albeit imperfectly, in later cases" (1949, 2). In fact, legal rules change from case to case and are remade in each case. These changes are an indispensable dynamic quality of law. Levi says:

> In an important sense legal rules are never clear, and, if a rule had to be clear before it could be imposed, society would be impossible. The mechanism accepts the differences of view and ambiguities of words. It provides for the participation of the community in resolving the ambiguity by providing a forum for the discussion of policy in the gap of ambiguity. . . . The mechanism is indispensable to peace in the community. (1949, 1)

Like modern law, missional theology seeks to formulate and communicate universal truth (cognitive), love (affective), and holiness (moral) in particular human contexts that are very diverse.[14] Like modern law, mis-

---

14. In seeking to develop a comprehensive model for understanding humans, Talcott Parsons, Edward Shills, Clyde Kluckhohn, and other leading social scientists (1952) speak of the three dimensions of persons, societies, and cultures: cognitive, affective, and evaluative. Theologically, these three dimensions are seen in the essence of God. He is light, love, and holy. The Enlightenment, seeking to attain objective truth, divorced truth, defined primarily by the sciences, from emotions and values because these introduced subjectivity and relegated them to the private spheres of life. Western Christianity continues to struggle with this divorce and tends to stress truth, aesthetic experiences, or morality rather than seeing them as different dimensions of a single whole.

sional theology must deal with human contexts that are ever changing. To assume that general rules, once properly determined, remain unchanged and need simply to be applied in later cases overlooks the changing nature of human life and the dynamic quality of theology that must be extended to new situations.

Finally, like modern law, missional theology must be done in a community that functions even when people do not agree completely. It needs structures that enable it to give meaning to ambiguities and to test constantly whether the community has come to deeper understanding of truth, love, and holiness, and how these are embodied in the individuals, societies, and cultures in this fallen world. The effort to find complete agreement before going to work is meaningless. It is to forget the very purpose for which theological reflection must be done, namely, to make known the gospel to humans in their contexts so that it can transform them.

Missiology

The final steps in missional methodology are to decide on a course of action in the specific case at hand and to carry it out. These must be biblically shaped and culturally sensitive. Too often, however, we stop the process at the point of dealing with immediate cases and do not use them to stimulate long-range reflection on the underlying issues and thereby to initiate procedures for discussing and dealing with them in the future. Specific cases should stimulate further reflection in systematic and biblical theologies that facilitate long-term, well-grounded responses to the social and cultural systems at hand.

The analogy to American law is not perfect. Missional theologians must go beyond the role of modern judges. We have divine revelation that shows us truth—how God, not we, sees things. But we must remember that our theologies are our human understanding of that revelation done by human beings using human languages and living in particular contexts; therefore, our theologies should never be equated one-to-one with divine revelation. We also have a mission to help the church and the world to move from where they are to where God wants them to be. This process of transformation includes individuals and corporate social and cultural systems. We cannot expect people simply to abandon their old ways and adopt new ones. They can move from where they are only by an ongoing process of transformation.

One strength of missional theology is its focus on mission. It takes humans seriously, in the particularity of their persons, societies, cultures, and ever-changing histories. It integrates cognition, affectivity, and evaluation in its response to biblical truth, and defines faith not simply as mental affirmations of truth or as positive experiences of God, but as beliefs and feelings that lead to response and obedience to the word of God. It rejects the division between pure and applied theology and sees ministry both as a way of doing theology and as a form of worship.

Missional theology also has its limitations. It begins by studying particular cases and people in the realities of their everyday lives. In doing so, it must develop theoretical and methodological ways of studying humans as individuals and societies, and the cultures they create. Here missiology can draw on the insights provided by the humanities and human sciences, but many of these are built on assumptions that omit or reject biblical foundations. It is important, therefore, for missional theologians to examine carefully the underlying premises of the theories and methods they use, just as systematic and biblical theologies must examine the theories and methods that inform their disciplines.

Complementarity

We need systematic, biblical, and missional theologies. To leave one of these out is to omit an essential dimension of the gospel. The first danger is reductionism. This assumes that two of these are secondary and can, ultimately, be reduced to one underlying theology. Biblical philosophers assume that if we have the correct systematic theology, the others will follow. Biblical theologians assume the same for biblical theology. Practicing missionaries and pastors assume that what we need are practical methods because we know the gospel and all we need is effective ways of communicating it.

A second approach is stratigraphic. We admit the importance of each of these theologies and study each separately, assuming that a proper knowledge of each will automatically lead, in practice, to their integration. There are two flaws in this approach. First, there is implicit in this a hierarchy in which one of the theologies is more foundational than the others. Second, true interdisciplinary dialogue and integration rarely take place, whether among individuals or in academic and ecclesiastical communities.

All three theologies are essential to understanding and living out the gospel, and they must be brought together. Given our human finiteness, we cannot (at least at this stage of our theological understanding) develop an overarching grand unifying theory that subsumes the three. Rather, we need to see that all three are essential and have their own identity and integrity, and that they complement and interact with one another (Grunbaum 1957; MacKay 1974). In missional theologizing, it is important that we draw on the understandings of systematic and biblical scholarship. Similarly, systematic and biblical scholarship must study the insights of missional theologians and their studies of human contexts, with all their diversity and particularities, in order to reexamine the questions they seek to answer and the categories and logics they use. They must deal with the questions that arise out of human lives and with the theories, methods, and answers people give to these questions.

It is important, therefore, that missionaries and missiologists study biblical and systematic theology to know the basic cognitive (truths), affective (love and beauty), and moral (holiness, righteousness) natures of the gospel. This informs their ministry and helps them draw on biblical and systematic theologians in dealing with specific cases. It is equally important that systematic and biblical theologians be trained in the theories and methods of the humanities and human sciences, so that they can understand the people they serve and the way they themselves are shaped by their own historical and sociocultural contexts. Otherwise theologians will answer questions people do not ask and be viewed as irrelevant, and they will not accurately distinguish what of the gospel they proclaim is from Scripture and what is from their sociocultural contexts. Moreover, they must help missiologists dealing with the bewildering array of particular issues that missiologists face in order to bring biblical critique to bear on them.

In the process of incarnating divine revelation in human contexts, we begin with classifications, methods, and theologies, and in the process we not only seek to communicate the gospel to humans in the particularities of their lives, but we also reexamine the classifications, methods, and theologies we use. In this process the classifications change as they are made, and theological understandings change as theology is applied (cf. Levi 1949, 4). In other words, our theologies and categories are open to examination and new insights even as we use them in life in an everchanging world. What keeps theologians of any kind from becoming the final arbiters of truth? In law (constitutional, statutory, and case) judges are accountable to a community of law that gives authority to the Constitution, statutes, and precedent cases.[15] In theology we must give

---

15. In law this raises the question of whether judges ultimately make the laws, because in interpreting the Constitution and statutes it is they who make the final decisions (Levi 1949). In modern law, however, they are bound by the Constitution, statutes, and precedent cases, and accountability to a community that appoints them and can overrule them.

ultimate authority to God and his revelation, given as it is through and to humans, and not to human understandings, which are always limited and approximate.

A complementary approach to drawing on systematic, biblical, and missional theologies recognizes that as humans we all live in and are shaped by particular cultural and historical contexts. We can begin only with our existing systems of thought. We must then consciously reflect not only on the task at hand but also on our questions, assumptions, methods, and theories in light of revelation and human realities. This reflection needs to be done by the community of theologians—including systematic, biblical, and missional theologians, because each can help correct one another's biases. This hermeneutical community should involve theologians from different cultures and from the past to correct cultural and historical biases. To build a bridge between universals and particulars, between past revelation and the gospel to the present, requires a continual dialogue among them all.

Cases

Two cases can help us understand missional theology and the methods it uses. The first is from Scripture, the second a hypothetical case from modern missions that draws on thousands of real cases.

Acts 15

The first major case is found in the early church and is recorded in Acts 15. The problem of neglecting the Hellenist widows had been handled by an administrative decision made by the council of the twelve apostles (Acts 6:1–2). Now a new problem arose that called into question the very identity of the church and threatened to split it apart. The crisis arose in Antioch, and the church there sent Barnabas, Paul, and others to present the case to the apostles and elders, who met to consider the matter (15:6). The question was clear: do Gentiles have to be circumcised and become practicing Jews before they are admitted into the church?

First the council gathered information from different witnesses on the events leading up to the crisis. The facts were clear. After persecution set in at Jerusalem, Philip went to preach to the Samaritans (8:4–25), and many were healed and believed. When the apostles heard about this they sent Peter and John to investigate. They reported back that the Holy

Spirit had indeed come and that these Samaritans could legitimately be considered new believers. Some may have argued that the Samaritans were half-Jews, and that God was gracious in letting them back in to the fold. Then Philip, claiming to be led by the Holy Spirit, baptized an Ethiopian (8:26–40). Some may have argued that he was a *God seeker* who had come from Jerusalem where he was probably looking into becoming a Jew through the prescribed process. But he was a eunuch, and eunuchs were not allowed into the temple. However, the Ethiopian resolved the problem himself by leaving the scene and not disturbing the status quo in the church. Then Peter witnessed to Cornelius (Acts 10), a godly man, but a full Gentile. This raised the anger of circumcised believers who criticized Peter when he came to Jerusalem. He had to explain himself to them at length. What could they say? Peter was one of the apostles, and who were they to challenge him? But then some unnamed people began to witness to the Hellenists in Antioch, and many of them and some Gentiles turned to the Lord and began to meet in fellowship together (11:19–21). The elders sent Barnabas to investigate, and he decided on the spot that God indeed was bringing Gentiles into the church. In fact, Barnabas and Paul had gone out on a mission journey and openly invited Gentiles to follow Christ and join the church. Now the matter had come to a head, and a decision was needed to resolve the problem.

There was little disagreement over the facts of the case. There was much disagreement on what should be done. All the parties involved argued their briefs before the council, each one seeking to persuade the elders that they were right (15:7). After Peter gave his closing statement, the assembly asked Barnabas and Paul to recount the most important facts relative to the issue. Then James announced the verdict. After citing Scripture to lay the foundation for theological reflection on the matter, he decided that a scriptural interpretation of the facts justified the admission of Gentiles into the church, and that without becoming Jews by circumcision and keeping the law. He then issued instructions on implementing the findings and urged Gentile converts, for the sake of maintaining unity, to abstain from behavior that was an unnecessary offense to the Jewish Christians. This was not a new law, but an exercise of their freedom in Christ to show love to their fellow Christians.

James and the elders, in fact, were doing missional theology. They began by studying the facts in the case and hearing arguments from various factions in the church. Then James used theological reflection to reach a decision and pass judgment based on the situation at hand.

A Case of Polygamy

A second case can help us understand the methods of missional theology. It comes from Africa (Hiebert and Hiebert 1987, 62–65), but the questions it raises are found around the world. What should the church do about polygamy, whether it be one man with many wives or one woman with many husbands?

The facts of this case are clear. Amadu is the chief of the village. When the missionaries came they asked him for permission to stay, and, out of hospitality, he allowed them to do so. After three years of ministry a small church of believers was formed, made up of two singles and five young couples, all monogamous. Having heard the gospel and witnessed its effects on new believers, Amadu came and wanted to be baptized into the church, along with his five wives. What should the church and missionaries do?

If, on the one hand, we turn first to systematic theology for an answer, we are in danger of passing judgment on situations we do not understand and, therefore, risk falling into blind legalism. If, on the other hand, we turn to biblical theology, the answer is more ambiguous. Many of the heroes of the Old Testament were polygamists, and there is no divine sanction of their actions. If we start with a careful study of the culture and the real life issues involved, we may come to an answer that is biblically based and culturally sensitive.

First, we need to examine the reasons for Amadu having five wives. The first was arranged by his family, because as the chief-to-be the matter is a political and social one. The first wife had no children, so Amadu took a second wife. It is imperative that a chief have an heir; a man's greatness is measured, in part, by having many descendants who remember and honor him. Amadu inherited two wives when his brother died. Each society must make provision for widows and orphans, and in Amadu's society it is the responsibility of a man to take care of his deceased brother's wives and children. This gives him the right to cohabit with them but, more importantly, it provides them with food, shelter, companionship, offspring, parenting, and role models. In his old age, as a renown chief, Amadu took a young wife to help at home and to add to his prestige.

Second, we need to look at the theological and sociocultural questions involved in the case. A few of these are as follows:

- Are traditional marriages true marriages or should Christians be remarried with Christian rites? In other words, are any of Amadu's marriages true marriages in the sight of God?

- Is polygamy (in this case polygyny) a sin?
- Is divorce a sin?
- Which is the greater sin—polygamy or divorce? If traditional marriages are true marriages and we ask Amadu to "put away" all but one wife, we teach monogamy but also divorce.
- If we ask Amadu to put away all but one wife, which one should he keep—his first, the mother of his children, one of those he inherited, or the youngest?
- If we ask Amadu to put away some wives and children, what will become of them? Often the women become prostitutes or both the women and the children are sold into slavery.
- Can the church baptize the wives of a polygamist? The wives are all monogamous, but if we baptize all of them the church will be made up largely of women.
- How should the church deal with the sins people commit before they become Christians?
- What are the evangelistic consequences of our decision? Forcing men to put away wives has been a great hindrance to the growth of the church.
- If Amadu is baptized with his wives, can he be a leader in the church (1 Tim. 3:2, 12)?
- Can a leader who is widowed remarry? Paul's instructions are that a leader is to be "a one-woman man." This can be interpreted as a prohibition of digamy—remarriage of a widower—as well as polygamy.
- Who should make the decision—the missionary, the young church, or the mission board?
- What should the missionaries do if their mission board has given them specific instructions not to baptize polygamists? They could be fired if they disobey.

The next step is to study Scripture for principles that determine our judgments. Here we should begin by studying how the character of God informs our judgment. God is a covenant keeper, so Amadu should honor the covenants he made, even though he made these before he became a Christian. God is compassionate, so the decision must take into account the wives and children, who are the real victims if they must be sent away. God is concerned that none should perish, so the judgment must be such that the door to forgiveness and salvation is open to all.

We should then examine specific issues that pertain to this case. There is no question that monogamy is God's ideal, but is polygamy a sin? And if so, what do we do with non-Christians who come with several wives? Is divorce a sin? And if so, how do we avoid making Amadu sin by divorcing wives to whom he is legitimately married so that he can be monogamous? After extended biblical studies, theologians such as Karl Barth find no compelling certainty that polygamy is a sin. The Old Testament makes no issue of it, and the instructions in the New Testament are for leaders in the church. Divorce, however, is condemned in both the Old and New Testaments.

Other issues must be decided. If we ask Amadu to put away all but one of his wives, what should Amadu or the church do for these women? Is it realistic for Amadu to continue to support them—including his own children—and not to treat them as wives? They will be looked down on and gossiped about. The young ones can have no children and will be condemned by a society in which women are honored for their children. And what will the church do with widows when the traditional solution has been rejected? Each of these, and many more issues, call for extended theological reflection.

We need also to look at how polygamy has been viewed throughout history. In the Old Testament little is said about it. In the New Testament Paul makes reference to it with regard to elders. The church in the West followed Greek morality and condemned polygamy outright. In modern mission history, missionaries from the West have traditionally required polygamists to put away all but one of their wives. The Lambeth Conference decreed the following:

> After we evaluate the case in the light of the findings of systematic theology, biblical theology, and church history, and of the ways other mission agencies have handled such cases in that and other parts of the world, we need to formulate principles that inform the case, make a decision, and provide ways in which to carry out the judgment and deal with its consequences.

We will not pass final judgment on the case here. Our purpose is to illustrate the methods of missional theology. What is clear is that a careful study of both Scripture and specific cases can help us apply biblical teachings to the realities of everyday life. It makes theology live for us, because theology is no longer an abstract understanding of truth but a map for living our lives.

Part 2

Exegeting Humans

3

Changing Images

Before I built a wall I'd ask to know
What was I walling in or walling out,
And to whom I was like to give offense.
Something there is that doesn't love a wall,
That wants it down.

—Robert Frost, "Mending Wall"

"We would rather have our daughter marry a non-Christian white than a Christian nonwhite." These were the words of white American evangelical parents who had grown up in the church. How can such sinful attitudes persist after generations of Christian teaching? Or are they sinful? And why does *race* matter when it comes to marriage, if two persons are both Christians and love each other? Our everyday relationships with other people are deeply shaped by how we see them—by who we think they are and who we think we are. But who are we? We must study human contexts in order to understand the nature of human identities.

Constructing Identities

In large measure, we are who our society says we are. We all live in communities made up of different kinds of people: women and men, tall and short, young and old, dark- and light-skinned, long- and short-nosed, poor and rich. Some of these differences are innate, others acquired. Most we ignore, or note only in passing. Others we highlight to organize our society. It is these that our society uses as markers to give us our identities as persons in social contexts. They define who we are and how we should behave. They set us apart from others and shape how we see and relate to them. In other words, our identities as persons and as groups of people and the expected relationships between us are social constructs.

Societies generally take note of social variables such as wealth, religion, and political views in creating identities and social categories. They also take note of biological variables, such as gender, and physical features, such as color and age, as markers. In the case of ethnic or racial identities, it is not the biological realities that determine the social categories we use to think and live with; rather, it is the biological markers our society takes note of and the categories it creates on the basis of these that give people their identities.

Social categories are built by establishing oppositions—by showing the differences between *us* and *others*. Each society and each age re-creates its Others in order to define itself. Edward Said notes that "far from a static thing then, identity of self or of 'other' is a much worked-over historical, social, intellectual, and political process that takes place as a contest involving individuals and institutions in all societies" (1995, 332).

Many social identities are hierarchically ordered. For example, class, caste, gender, and ethnicity are generally ranked, with the powerful at the top. For the most part, it is those who have the power to define the categories and impose these on a society as a whole who define themselves as being more "human," "advanced," and "superior." Over time, people come to see these categories as innately real because they shape and explain their collective experiences. Those who are excluded and oppressed have their own views of who they are, but these views are generally ignored by the dominant community.

One of a person's primary sociopsychological identities is ethnicity—the feeling that she or he is part of a group because the members are the "same kind" of people. This *consciousness of kind* is based on the belief that the group shares the same inherited characteristics. Often these are thought to be "based on a myth of collective ancestry, which usually carries with it traits believed to be innate" (Horowitz 1985, 52). In other words, members may be said to share the same blood. Often ethnicity is associated with language, religion, and particular cultural practices that form a common heritage. One or more of these markers may serve as sources of ethnic divisiveness that lead to disdain, discrimination, accusations of inferior ancestry, and violence among ethnic groups.

Racism is an extreme form of ethnocentrism that is particularly oppressive. Fredrickson writes:

> It originates from a mindset that regards "them" as different from "us" in ways that are permanent and unbridgeable. This sense of difference provides a motive or rationale for using our power advantage to treat the ethno-racial Other in ways that we would regard as cruel or unjust if applied to members of our own group. (2002, 9)

In other words, racism is what happens when ethnicity is seen as biologically inherent and hierarchically organized.

Both ethnic hostility and racism shape and are shaped by how people see and relate to Others they encounter in everyday life, but there is much more to them than this. They are institutionalized in social and cultural structures of domination that divide peoples into different categories on the basis of what are thought to be unalterable characteristics. An analysis of how Euro-Americans have viewed Others can help us study the complex structures that make up ethnocentrism and racism. In this chapter I draw on McGrane (1989), and look at some of the historical forces that have shaped the way Europeans and North Americans have viewed Others during the past few centuries and how these perceptions led to the racism that now plagues our societies. We then examine ways to change our perceptions of Others in order to build bridges of understanding and love between us.

European Encounters with Others and Otherness

People have always had stereotypes of their Others. In the sixteenth century, Sebastian Münster described the Scots as faithful and vengeful people; the Jews, prudent but envious; the Persians, steadfast but disloyal; the Egyptians, stable and crafty; the Greeks, wise but deceitful; and the Spaniards, drunken, violent, and sophisticated. In 1527, Henry Agrippa declared, "In singing also the Italians bleat, the Spaniards Whine, the Germans Howl, and the French Quaver" (Harris 1968, 399–400).

During the High Middle Ages educated Europeans often imagined foreigners in two categories. The first was monster. North Europeans had many stories of humanoids who lived in the forests and prairies, and were embodiments of evil forces (Jeffrey 1980). They spoke of *satyr* (half-human and half-goat), *pyrs* (hairy woodmen), water sprites, the Old Norse *îviôr*, the Scandinavian *bergrisar*, trolls living under bridges, giants in mountain castles, ogres, and werewolves. In Christianity, these monsters were sometimes said to be descendants of Cain. The second category was infidel. Muslim armies had taken Palestine and were in Spain and attacking Vienna. They were clearly humans, but they were infidels because they had heard the gospel and rejected it. Therefore, they had to be driven back and killed. The result was, at least in part, the Crusades.

The Age of Exploration (1500–1700)

European perceptions of the world changed radically at the end of the fifteenth century. Explorers seeking new routes to the spicelands of India discovered unknown lands and strange people not found on their maps. The age was one of exploration and of redrawing physical and mental maps to include hitherto unknown lands and peoples.

Europe's encounter with Others during the Age of Exploration raised profound questions. Who were these Others? Were they human? Did they have souls that needed to be saved? Could they be enslaved and killed, or was this murder? The encounter with new peoples raised questions not only of geography but also of sociology, economics, politics, and theology.

The Western commercial world saw the newly discovered Others as a source of goods and labor—of gold and slaves. European exploration was not random. The explorers were looking *for* something: namely spices, gold, and labor. But what right did Europeans have to enslave other peoples? Many argued that these Others were like children. Therefore the Europeans were justified in colonial expansion in which they acted as parents, educating and managing the natives' wealth for the natives' own good (McGrane 1989).

The Christian response was that these people were truly humans. If so, how should Christians relate to them? Were they children of Adam and Eve? If so, they needed salvation. If not, they might be humans untouched by the fall. The church concluded that these people were sinners in need of salvation, and the descendants of Adam and Eve. They were neither Christian heretics who distorted the gospel nor Muslim infidels who rejected it. They had not heard the gospel. They were "pagans" and "heathens" who were potential Christians. The result was the birth of the modern mission movement, first by the Roman Church and later by Protestants.

Scientists took a different view of these Others. Science was becoming increasingly secular. The earth of the fifteenth century was seen as an island (*orbis terrarum*) made up of Europe, Asia, and Africa, with the Holy City of Jerusalem in the center and God in control. This sacred space was surrounded by the dark, inhuman, evil void of the deep waters. Crossing the seas and discovering new lands radically changed the way Europeans viewed the earth. Now, for the first time, the world was seen as a uniform, continuous, secular space covered by continents and oceans. In this new world, Others were no longer "fallen" and in need of redemption. They were secular humans who could be compared with other humans. In these comparisons they were viewed as "barbarians" and "savages." It was Western explorers who named and studied Others and their lands.

The Age of Enlightenment (1700–1930)

The definition of the Others changed with the coming of the Enlightenment. The shift is epitomized in the experiences of Robinson Crusoe, the leading character in Daniel Defoe's novel, *Robinson Crusoe* (1719). Crusoe was the quintessential Enlightenment man—solitary individual, Cartesian rationalist, and technological inventor (McGrane 1989, 44). After almost eighteen years alone on an island, he came across charred human bones on a beach. "Cannibals!" he thought. From the depth of his European body and soul he vomits. His initial reaction was that these were beasts, savages, evil—a response that fit the Age of Exploration. By contrast, he was human and good.

Crusoe initially decides to slaughter all the savages he can, but—on further reflection—his worldview begins to shift. He writes:

> What authority or call had I to pretend to be judge and executioner upon these men as criminals, whom Heaven had thought fit for so many ages to suffer unpunished to go on. . . . It is certain these people do not commit this as a crime; it is not against their own consciences reproving or their light reproaching them. (Defoe 1961, 168)

Crusoe decides that it is wrong for him to judge other people by *his* standards. They must be judged in light of *their own* morality and culture. But it is clear that his culture is more advanced, and these people need to be taught true morality.

When Crusoe rescues one of the cannibals, the cannibal places his own neck under Crusoe's foot, voluntarily subordinating himself to Crusoe. Rather than ask his name, Crusoe exercises the sovereign right of the explorer and names him—he is Friday, and he will address Crusoe as

Master. Thereby Crusoe transforms the stranger from a nameless *savage* who exists beyond the boundaries of humanity and civilization into Friday, a *primitive human being* who is a subordinate member in Crusoe's world. Crusoe teaches Friday to speak English and gives him a place to live halfway between Crusoe's house and the forest inhabited by beasts and cannibals. Friday is awestruck by Crusoe's gun and wants to worship it. Crusoe teaches him that it is not miraculous and that it can be explained in natural terms.

In their daily encounters, Crusoe is increasingly forced to recognize Friday's full humanity. How, then, can Crusoe account for the differences between them? His answer is that Friday is unenlightened, therefore naked, primitive, and non-Christian, while he is enlightened, clothed, and Christian. But Friday can be taught and saved through Crusoe's efforts. Typical of Enlightenment mentality, there is no mention of what Friday thought of Crusoe or of Crusoe's attempts to "civilize" him. In the Enlightenment imagination, as seen in Daniel Defoe's novel, Others will naturally wish to subordinate themselves to Europeans.

Crusoe illustrates the transition from medieval thought to the world of the Enlightenment. Three fundamental shifts marked this change in the popular and scientific worlds. First, Others were no longer savages, but unenlightened; evil was no longer sin, it was ignorance. The earlier distinction between refined Christian versus idolatrous savage was replaced by the *civilized* European versus the superstitious, ignorant *primitive*.

Second, in time the Others became "aboriginals." They represented humans who had not evolved as those who lived in the West. These Others still lived in the Stone Age. They were living fossils. But if these Others are now like European ancestors once were, they help modern people understand their own story. Joseph Conrad captures this view in his description of Africa:

> We penetrated deeper and deeper into the heart of darkness. . . . But suddenly as we struggled around a bend, there would be a glimpse of peaked grass roofs, a burst of yells, a whirl of black limbs, a mass of hands, clapping, of feet stomping, of bodies swaying. . . . It was unearthly, and the men were—No, they were not inhuman. . . . They howled and leaped . . . but what thrilled you was just the thought of their humanity—like yours—the thought of your remote kinship. (1950, 105)

Euro-Americans of the time saw the world as a great museum (McGrane 1989). In the Amazon they saw their remotest ancestors; in New Guinea, they saw stage two, and so on. The people of the world revealed *their* history, and the only audience that could understand the play was, of course, "them." They had the benefit of hindsight: they knew how the story ended; they *were* how the story ended. It was clear to scientists that Western civilization was the most evolved of all cultures. Viewed this way, the colonial venture was not oppressive. It was the benevolent efforts of enlightened people to help the Others join them in their full humanity.

But there remained in the minds of some a gnawing doubt. Was it possible that savages were Noble Savages who were happier than modern humans? Herman Melville captured this doubt in his description of the encounter of a French admiral and a native king.

> The admiral came forward with uncovered head and extended one hand, while the old king saluted him by a stately flourish of his weapon. The next moment they stood side by side, these two extremes of the social scale—the polished Frenchman, and the poor tattooed savage. . . . At what an immeasurable distance, thought I, are these two beings removed from each other! In the one is shown the result of long centuries of progressive refinement, which have gradually converted the mere creature into the semblance of all that is elevated and grand; while the other, after the lapse of the same period, has not advanced one step in the career of improvement. "Yet after all," quoth I to myself, "insensible as he is to a thousand wants, and removed from harassing cares, may not the savage be the happier man of the two?" (1974, 33)

The third shift was that the Others became Children. They could be enlightened through education by Western parents and teachers. This justified the subordination of social Others, the colonization of the world to bring light to those who were trapped in darkness and ignorance.

At the heart of the Enlightenment was science, which was assumed by most modern people to provide objective and true knowledge. They believed that science had discovered differences that exist in nature itself. The way science defined things had an aura of reality and truthfulness about it that traditional taxonomies did not. Science told people how things *really were*.

The success of biology in studying nature opened the door for the scientific study of humans. In 1735, Carl Linnaeus included humans as a species in the primate genus and tried to divide humans into varieties. This opened the way for scientific racism, which saw humans as part of the animal kingdom rather than as children of God endowed with spiritual capacities other creatures do not have (Fredrickson 2002, 57). In 1863, the Ethnological

Society in England split over the question of whether human beings were "of one blood" or different species descended from different primates. The Anthropological Society of London held that Negroes were a different species from Europeans (Reining 1970, 5). By the end of the century, however, anthropologists affirmed the biological unity of human beings. Christians argued, on the basis of Genesis, that all humans were of one kind.

But, having agreed that humans were one species, the study of race became a central object of scientific study. People were not humans to be known personally. They were objects to be counted, analyzed, and reduced to general categories, laws, and theories. They were lumped into anonymous collectives in which particularities were eliminated by definition and broad generalizations formulated. The result was the theory of racial determinism and modern racism.

Science organized races, like it did all animal species, in terms of a hierarchy. Rudyard Kipling captures this view of life. "Mule, horse, elephant, or bullock, he obeys his driver, and the driver his sergeant, and the sergeant his lieutenant, and the lieutenant his captain, and the captain his major, and the major his colonel, and the colonel his brigadier commanding three regiments, and the brigadier his general, who obeys the Viceroy, who is the servant of the Empress" (quoted in Said 1995, 45). With regard to race, the categories were ranked along a hierarchy from inferior to superior, from dark to light skin, from curly to straight hair, from little to much body hair. This was used to justify conquest, colonialism, and slavery. The inferiors must be treated as inferiors. In colonialism this led to stereotypes and rationalizations:

> The natives are lazy; they do not respond like civilized men to the offer of wages; they need to be taught the virtues of civilized forms of labor by means other than those appropriate to civilized man. . . . Being more childlike than Europeans, it is dangerous for natives to have free access to alcoholic drinks. . . . Such people, if given a chance, prefer to walk rather than to ride, they like to sleep on the cold ground rather than on warm beds; they work in the rain without feeling wet, work in the sun without feeling hot, and carry loads on their heads without getting tired. Life is not so dear in these people as to Europeans; when their children die, they are not so deeply disturbed and when they themselves suffer injury, it does not hurt as much as it does it the civilized man. (Harris 1968, 135).

The dominant community created racial categories and imposed these on the powerless. Moreover, the powerful used defining characteristics that favored themselves over the Others. It was whites who defined and named themselves and named Others *nonwhites* and *colored*. Whites studied non-whites; not the other way around. Because whites were doing the studying, they assigned what they saw as their characteristics to the highest rank. Euro-Americans were the normal humans, the standard against which the Others were measured. They were Occidental, civilized, law-abiding. The opposite characteristics were assigned to their Others: Others were Oriental, uncivilized, primitive, and ruled by passions, not reason. In so doing, whites defined themselves over against their Others. Their classifications reinforced the sense of the otherness of the Others, particularly since that otherness was defined in terms of what were seen as innate, unchangeable characteristics, and overlooked similarities and commonalities among peoples.

Some scientists argued that even though some races are inferior, they could be perfected and made potentially equal to the higher races. Given enough time and teaching, the inferior races could be civilized and come to resemble their European conquerors. This led to notions of the "white man's burden." Many who argued against slavery in the United States did so not on the basis of the equality of all humans but on the humanitarian argument that the inferior should be helped, not enslaved, by the superior. Christians such as Count J. A. De Gobineau argued that people from other races could be converted because Christianity appeals to the lowly and simple; it could be understood and accepted by the lowest types of humans. But, he argued, this does not mean that in other matters they are equal to Europeans.

But racial identities were also contested. The powerless had their own classifications and definitions of themselves, even though in public life they had to live with the definitions of themselves given them by the dominant community. The powerless lived with a tension in terms of who they really were. The dominant community had no such crisis. Its members were secure and comfortable in their identity. In fact, they often saw no problem with racism and assumed that because there was no problem with racism then it was simply the way of things, and they were doing well by showing kindness to Others.

Scholarly classification helped create a particularly virulent type of racism. What counts in racism is not so much what people are or think, but what they are shaped to be and to think. Social identities are not only mental images of self and other; they are social constructs based on contests involving concrete political issues such as immigration laws, legislation of personal conduct, legitimization of violence, the content of education, and the direction of foreign policy. For Europeans, the result was colonialism in which Others were ruled in order to improve their lot in life by making them more like Euro-Americans. The West defined all Others, reconstructed their histories, and determined how they should progress. In the end, two-thirds of the world was ruled by a few European countries. The inequality of races and the necessary domination of the many by the few were assumed by the end of the nineteenth century.

In the end, such classifications and hierarchies dehumanize Others; they are objects to be studied and controlled, not humans to relate to. George Orwell writes:

> When you walk through a town like this—two hundred thousand inhabitants, of whom at least twenty thousand own literally nothing except the rags they stand up in—when you see how the people live, and still more, how easily they die, it is difficult to believe that you're walking among human beings. All colonial empires are in reality founded upon that fact. The people have brown faces—besides they have so many of them! Are they really the same flesh as yourself? Do they even have names? Or are they merely a kind of undifferentiated brown stuff, about as individual as bees or coral insects? They arise out of the earth, they sweat and starve for a few years, and then they sink back into the nameless mounds of the graveyard and nobody notices that they are gone. And even the graves themselves soon fade back into the soil. (1956, 251)

The Enlightenment deeply influenced Christian whites in the West. Christians led the fight against slavery and human exploitation. They were also shaped by the world around them. Enlightenment attitudes were used to justify segregated churches and even slavery. They supported the mission movement and saw whites as uniquely called to propagate Christianity and civilization around the world (Taber 1991). Missionaries sacrificed their lives to bring the gospel to people around the world, but many took for granted the racial superiority of whites and opposed intermarriage with the *natives*. Henry Venn, a leading missionary to India, wrote that the white missionary was "another and superior race than his converts" (see Taber 1991, 62).

All this must be said, but as Sanneh (1993) points out, many of the missionaries were concerned with communicating the gospel to other peoples. They lived with the people and often defended them against oppression by business and government. Moreover, by translating the Bible into native languages, communicating to them a universal gospel, and baptizing the converts into the global church, the missionaries dignified the people and helped them more than other Westerners did to preserve their cultural identities.

The Age of Post-Enlightenment (1930–)

The Enlightenment reached its peak at the end of the nineteenth century. Two world wars and the rise of anticolonial and nativistic movements began to call the Enlightenment project into question. Moreover, prolonged encounters with people in other cultures led Westerners, in their encounters with Others, to increasingly see them as fully human and their cultures as having much worth. Even Crusoe came to see Friday increasingly as human.

To acknowledge the full humanity of other peoples raised a new question: how could the Others be equal to us and yet remain Other? Enlightenment scholars studied people from their scientific point of view. Now they tried to see the world through the eyes of the people they were studying. The Others now became *natives*. Others were no longer primitive. They were fully rational beings having their own autonomous cultures. The word *civilization* associated with a hierarchical view of peoples was rejected in favor of *culture*, in which all are different but equal. Cultures are now seen as unique and autonomous. Each is seen as discrete, bounded, and self-contained, and each functions to maintain a harmonious society. Cultures are also seen as morally neutral. People in one culture should not judge other cultures. To do so is ethnocentric and imperialistic.

This post-Enlightenment view of Others is an important corrective to the arrogance and oppressions of the past, but it leaves Others as simply *others*. There is an insurmountable wall between Us and Them. In a world of diversity, the question is: how can people of different communities build a world of harmony, justice, and love? The underlying notion that race is natural, stable, and inherent is false. Identities are not natural and stable but constructed and contested. But to say that human realities are constantly being made and unmade is unsettling and leads to fear. Reactions to this fear lead to patriotism, xenophobia, and chauvinism. Said asks:

> Can one divide human reality, as human reality seems to be genuinely divided, into clearly different cultures, histories, traditions, societies, even races, and survive the consequences humanly? By surviving the consequences humanly, I mean to ask whether there is any way of avoiding the hostility expressed by the division, say, of men into "us" . . . and "they." (1995, 45)

A Christian View of Others

Christians must address the issues of racism, injustice, and hostility and show how humans of different kinds can live together in peace and justice, or the gospel becomes good news only for a few: the powerful. We must address the sin of racism in the church. Too often we have been influenced more by the world in which we live than by the Word of God. We must not see others as savages, primitives, or irreconcilably other. How then should we view Others?

The Oneness of Humanity

First, Christians must constantly reaffirm the biblical teaching that at the deepest level of identity all humans are one. On the surface they are male and female; black, brown, and white; rich and poor; old and young, but underneath these differences they are all fully human. This oneness of humanity is declared in the creation account (Gen. 1:26) and affirmed by the universalism implicit in the Old Testament (Gen. 12; Ps. 67; 72:17; 148:11–13; Isa. 11:10; 19:23–25; 45:22; 56:7; 60:3; 66:18; Jer. 4:2; 33:9; Mic. 4:1–2; Hag. 2:7). In Christ and in the New Testament the implications of this common humanity are worked out more fully.

In affirming the oneness of humanity, Christians must not deny the great difficulty in understanding people in other cultures. It is easy to say that we love them when we have few deep relationships with other people. Far too often we claim to know what others are thinking and feeling, when, in fact, we may be totally wrong. The more people study cultural differences, the more they realize how difficult it is to see Others as humans like themselves and to build deep interethnic relationships of mutuality and love, but the more they see the necessity to do so.

The Oneness of Christians

Scripture leads to a second conclusion: in the church believers are members of one new people (*ethnos*). In Christ, God's kingdom has come to earth (Matt. 4:17–25). A new age is at hand. The church is the sign and manifestation of that kingdom, and all who follow Jesus as their Lord become members of a new people. Stott writes, "For the sake of the glory of God and the evangelization of the world, nothing is more important than that the church should be, and should be seen to be, God's new society" (1979, 10).

Peter, when he went to the house of Cornelius, learned that the church is a new community, not based on the old identities of this world. Peter's amazement at what was taking place can be detected in the words he spoke in the house of Cornelius: "Truly I perceive that God shows no partiality" (Acts 10:34 RSV).

For Paul, unity and living as fellow citizens in the new kingdom are the way the church demonstrates that it is indeed the church. In his letter to the Ephesians, Paul describes the hostilities that divide humans (2:11–12), shows how Christ brought those hostilities to an end (2:13–18), and argues that Christians united in Christ are God's object lesson to the world (2:19–22). Paul writes, "[Christ] tore down the wall we used to keep each other at a distance. . . . Then he started over. Instead of continuing with two groups of people separated by centuries of animosity and suspicion, he created a new kind of human being, a fresh start for everyone" (Eph. 2:14–15 Message). It should come as no surprise that in the churches Paul planted, Jews, Greeks, barbarians, Thracians, Egyptians, and Romans were able to feel at home. This mutual acceptance of Jews and Gentiles in the church was itself a testimony to the world of the transforming power of the gospel. Paul says that in Christ, Christians *are* one body (Eph. 4:4). If they are not part of the body, they are not a part of Christ.

This unity of a shared new life in Christ bridges the human distinctions of ethnicity (Gal. 2:11–21), class (1 Cor. 10:11), and gender (Gal. 3:28; Acts 2:44–47; 4:32). Rader writes, "Ephesians sees the church as the community in which the deepest hostility between men was healed. . . . When the church views herself in the light of Ephesians 2:11–22 then it is impossible for her to be conformed to the divisions which exist in society. It is her nature to be the place where divisions are healed" (1978, 253, 255). The importance of the unity and fellowship within the church is seen in Christ's high priestly prayer. On the eve of his death, Jesus is not concerned for himself but for his followers. He prays, "I have given them the glory that you gave me, that they may be one as we are one: I in them and you in me. May they be brought to complete unity to let the world know that you sent me and have loved them even as you have loved me" (John 17:22–23 NIV). The unity of the church is not a by-product of the good news; it is an essential part of the gospel.

During this time when the kingdom of God has come but is not in its fullness, Christians continue to live in two worlds, in the kingdoms of this world and in the kingdom of God. The former is temporary, the latter eternal. The identities of Christians in this world (the old *aeon*) are relativized because they are passing away. The Christian's new identity as a member in the family of Christ is eternal and takes precedence over all earthly identities.

Tearing Down Walls of Racism

If races and racism are socially constructed, they can be deconstructed. To do so, however, is not easy. Christians must deal with both our personal perceptions of ourselves and others and the social systems in which we live that divide people into hostile groups. To start with, we must examine our own attitudes toward race and racism. We then must work to transform the sociocultural systems that perpetuate racism—to bring about reconciliation, love, and peace among the people of the world.

To deal with perceptions of ourselves and others, Christians must begin examining our understanding of our own social identities. We are daughters and sons, husbands and wives, mothers and fathers, teachers and students, pastors and parishioners, merchants and customers, Chinese, Nigerians, Native Americans, African Americans, Hispanics, and Anglo Americans. We activate each identity in appropriate social contexts. We do not act as husband or wife to students in class, or as teachers to presidents of the United States.

We must also examine how we prioritize these social identities. Some are primary; some are more surface identities. One person may be a male-motorcyclist-American-Democrat, in that order. Another may be a Baptist-mother-teacher-gardener. When identities come into conflict, people choose one identity at the expense of the others. For example, when the Christian parents said they would rather have their child marry a non-Christian white than a Christian nonwhite, they were saying that their ethnic identity was deeper than their Christian identity (fig. 3.1).

Christians must learn to see our primary identity as human beings. When we meet Others, we must see them first as fellow humans, and only secondarily as males or females, Americans or Arabs, rich or poor. In reaching out to the lost, Christians must meet them at the deepest level of their common humanity.

Christians must also learn to see our primary identity as Christians. When we meet other Christians, we must see them as brothers and sisters

FIGURE 3.1
Levels of Identity

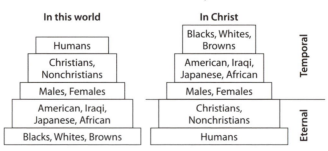

in the same family. This belonging to a new community is our eternal identity. Our oneness with other Christians is deeper than the identities that divide us on earth, such as ethnicity (Jew or Gentile), class (slave or free), and gender (male or female), which are not eternal. In the church, at least, Christians should manifest this eternal reality and not be captive to the world around them.

How can Christians learn to see their world this way? We cannot expect new believers to immediately put their new identity in Christ at the deepest level of their hierarchy of identities. Learning to see others as truly humans and as members of the same family must be an intentional part of all discipling processes. Christians must begin by seeking relationships with people outside our circles. We must learn how to build relationships with Others by asking others about themselves and seeking to learn to know them rather than talking about ourselves. We need to build multiethnic fellowships and work to break down the walls that divide us. Our churches must model the oneness of the body of Christ. New Christians must be led to deal with their racism, for it is sin. It divides the body of Christ and closes the door to effective witness to nonbelievers. And all this must be modeled by those who are mature in faith.

But Christians must do more than tear down the walls that divide people so deeply. We need to celebrate our oneness and build relationships of unity and love. If our primary identities are ethnic, cultural, and national, we may gather for worship and fellowship, but we know that when tensions arise, these underlying differences will divide us, and we will be ready to war against one another. If, on the contrary, "human" and "Christian" are our primary identities, we can celebrate ethnic, gender, and cultural differences, knowing that when problems arise we will remain united.

Unity in the body of Christ does not rest in uniformity but in the common *blood* that Christians have in Christ. We may disagree and quarrel, but nothing takes away our common identity. Unity in the church that breaks down walls of ethnicity, gender, and class takes place wherever Christ is Lord of our lives. Yancey writes:

> A society that welcomes people of all races and social classes, that is characterized by love and not polarization, that cares most for its weakest members, that stands for justice and righteousness in a world enamored with selfishness and decadence, a society in which members compete for the privilege of serving one another—this is what Jesus meant by the kingdom of God. (1995, 253)

4

Early Anthropology

Despite the history of racism, anthropology has been a valuable discipline in the study of missiology. Yet, the relationship between anthropologists and missionaries has been that of half-siblings—drawing one another on and frequently quarreling. Both work with people abroad. Both struggle with the questions of Others and otherness. Many anthropologists have lived with and obtained some of their field data from missionaries, often without acknowledging their sources, and missionaries have benefitted from anthropological findings. Nevertheless, the relationship between them has remained strained (Salmone 1986). Like other academic studies, including biblical and systematic theologies, anthropology began as a Western discipline and as a project of the Enlightenment (Barnard 2000). During the past hundred years, anthropologists have developed different theories to understand humans and, in varying degrees, missionaries have drawn on their insights in their ministries. Like other Western disciplines, these theories have cast light on the understanding of humans, but they are also culturally situated and so have their own limitations and biases.

The introduction of anthropology to missiology raises a critical question: how can the findings of anthropology be integrated into missions while retaining solid biblical foundations? This question is not unique to

Portions of this chapter appeared previously in "The Social Sciences and Missions: Applying the Message," in *Missiology and the Social Sciences: Contributions, Cautions and Conclusions*, ed. Edward Rommen and Gary Corwin (Pasadena, CA: William Carey Library, 1996).

the incorporation of anthropology. It underlies much of the discussion surrounding the inclusion of psychology in training ministers and Christian counselors, the integration of medical sciences and Christian healing in pastoral care, and the use of modern business sciences in the administration of the church and its institutions. It also underlies discussions about the use of Greek categories and reasoning in systematic theology and of historiography in biblical theology and church history, because these, too, are rooted in Western research traditions. Can young churches around the world engage in systematic theology using other logics? To what extent is biblical theology captive to modern critical historiography (Frykenberg 1996)?

Remembering Larry Laudan's point that a discipline is defined not by the answers it gives but by the questions it raises, the data it examines, and the methods it legitimates, we can say that anthropology asks the question: what is the nature of humans and their systems? The data it examines is human thought and behavior around the world. The methods it legitimates are observation, participation, interviews, cases, questionnaires, and other "empirical" ways of gathering information. In short, anthropology is the study of humans in all their dimensions and contexts throughout history.

At the deepest level anthropology, like all disciplines, is embedded in a worldview—a set of cognitive, affective, and normative assumptions about the nature of reality. As its worldview changes, the discipline undergoes theoretical shifts from one school of thought to another. Thomas Kuhn (1970) points out that these schools of thought compete for acceptance and, over time, cause changes to take place in the lower-level theorizing that is done, not to mention the interpretation of facts on the ground. We must ask: What are the anthropological paradigms that have shaped missiology? How have these shaped the way we think about and do missions? And how do they stand up under biblical critique? In this chapter we look at only a few of the paradigms that have emerged from anthropology to see how they have shaped Protestant missions.[1] Anthropology and modern missions were both born during the era of modernity, and both have been affected by the rise of late or postmodernity, and, more recently, of glocalism (see chapter 5).

1. Catholic missiology has a long history of interaction with anthropology. During the evolutionary period, the Vienna School, led by Father Schmidt and Father Grabner, played a leading role in showing that the majority of simple tribal societies have the concept of a high god, thereby discrediting the prevailing theory that the high god and monotheism were late in the evolution of religion. Later Louis Luzbetack (1988) played a key role in giving Catholic missiology solid anthropological foundations.

Modernity

From the fourth-century triumph of Christianity in the Roman Empire, through the Middle Ages and the Reformation, the Western mind was, above all, theistic. Virtually without question, all life and nature were assumed to be under the care of a personal God whose intentions toward humans were pure, and whose power to implement these intentions was unlimited. Huston Smith writes:

> In such a world, life was transparently meaningful. But although men understood the purpose of their lives, it does not follow that they understood, or even presumed to be capable of understanding the dynamics of the natural world. . . . Not until the high Middle Ages was a Christian cosmology attempted, and then through Greek rather than Biblical inspiration, following the rediscovery of Aristotle's *Physics* and *Metaphysics*. . . . We can summarize the chief assumptions underlying the Christian outlook by saying they held that reality is focused in a person, that the mechanics of the physical world exceed our comprehension, and that the way to our salvation lies not in conquering nature but in following the commandments which God has revealed to us. (1982, 5–6)

The Renaissance interest in the early Greeks revived the Hellenic dualism of natural/supernatural and the focus on nature. It reintroduced Greek intrinsic sets and abstract algorithmic logic as the methods to study it. Humans began to look at their environment instead of beyond it. The result was modern science. With diligent research, nature was brought into focus as a coherent, law-abiding system that is intelligible.

In this process, God was not entirely eclipsed. Smith notes:

> Rather, God was eased toward thought's periphery. Not atheism but deism, the notion that God created the world but left it to run according to its own inbuilt laws, was the Modern Mind's distinctive religious stance. God stood behind nature as its creator, but it was through nature that his ways and will were known. (1982, 7)

The modern outlook had three controlling presuppositions: first, reality is ordered by impersonal natural and moral laws; second, human reason is capable of discerning this order; and third, the path to human fulfillment lies in discovering these laws and using them to improve human life on earth.

At the heart of modernity was rationalism, the belief that human minds properly used could discover the truth. Smith writes:

Rationalism had entered theology as early as the Middle Ages, but as long as the Christian outlook prevailed, final confidence was reserved for the direct pronouncements of God himself as given in Scripture. In the modern period, God's existence came to stand or fall on whether reason, surveying the order of nature, endorsed it. It was as if Christendom and God himself awaited the verdict of science and the philosophers. . . . By including God within a closed system of rational explanation, modernism lost sight of the endless qualitative distinction between God and man. (1982, 11–12)

The world increasingly was viewed as a clock and God as the clockmaker, who finished his work and left it to run on its own.

The dominant worldview assumptions of an age color the thoughts and actions of the men and women who live in it. Like a pair of glasses through which we look, they are largely unnoticed. They are what we think with, not what we think about. But they shape the ways we see the world: our understanding of truth, our sense of right and wrong, what we think it means to be a man or woman, how we worship God, or whether we have a God to worship (Smith 1982, 4). It should not surprise us, therefore, that modernity profoundly shaped both missions and anthropology, and the relationship between them.

Anthropology and Missions in the Early Modern Years

The discovery of a new world populated by previously unknown creatures raised profound theological, economic, political, and scientific questions. Were these creatures human and in need of salvation? Could they be enslaved or ruled? And what accounted for their diversity? Two movements in particular addressed these questions. The academic community's response was anthropology—the science of Others and otherness. The church's response was missions—ministry to these Others.

The history of the relationship between missions and anthropology is a long and checkered one. As Conrad Reining has shown (1970), anthropology in England had its origins in the active mission and humanitarian movements of the early nineteenth century that arose, in part, out of the Wesleyan revivals. One of these, the Society for the Abolition of Slavery, arose in defense of the slaves. After the Emancipation Act of 1833 ended slavery in England, the abolitionists turned their attention to the welfare of native peoples in the colonial dependencies. In 1838 they organized the Aborigines Protection Society in London. Soon after its establishment, the society split over the question of how best to help the natives. One faction, including many of the missionaries, wanted to protect the rights of the aborigines by giving them immediately the privileges of Western civilization, such as education, medicine, and the gospel. The other faction wanted to study the people in order to understand them better and to protect them from Western incursion. The latter group organized the Ethnological Society of London in 1843 for the study of human biological diversity.

In the late nineteenth century, anthropology emerged in the universities as an academic discipline focused on the study of people, their societies, and their cultures. Despite their different purposes, at this time the relationship between missionaries and anthropologists was not hostile. Many missionaries, such as John Williams, Lorimer Fison and George Turner in Melanesia, and C. V. Wiser in India, played key roles in the development of ethnology, working closely with anthropologists and publishing penetrating studies on non-Western cultures. Many anthropologists depended on missionaries who resided in the areas they studied for ethnographic data and analysis. R. H. Codrington, one of the early great missionaries and ethnographers, wrote: "When a European has been living for two or three years among strangers, he is sure to be fully convinced that he knows all about them; when he has been ten years or so amongst them, if he is an observant man, he finds that he knows very little about them, and so begins to learn" (1891, vii). Hence, in the beginning anthropologists did not seriously contest missionary purposes, and missionaries contributed much to ethnology.

The Theory of Evolution (1840–1930)

The first grand unifying theory to emerge in the academy sought to explain the diversity of human beings both biologically and culturally, using a secular variation of the biblical story. The theory of evolution affirmed that meaning is found in a grand metanarrative that moves from simple beginnings to the complex present-day world, ending—hopefully—in an earthly utopia. But it held that man—not God—is the measure of all things. Darwin developed a theory of biological evolution. Comte proposed a theory of cultural evolution from savagery to barbarism to civilization. Taken together, these theories formed a secular history designed to explain human history and diversity. It incorporated all humans into one cosmic story of progress from simple to complex, from primitive to civilized, from prelogical to logical. The superiority of Western peoples, science, and technology was self-evident and legitimized Western domination of the rest of the world.

Biological Evolution

The central question in anthropology from 1840 to 1900 had to do with the great biological diversity among humans. Missionaries, on the basis of Genesis 1, affirmed the biological unity of all human beings and the need to bring the gospel to all of them. Anthropologists split over the issue of human origins. In 1863, the Anthropological Society of Britain broke from the Ethnological Society, arguing that Africans and other "natives" were descended from primates lower than Europeans. Because of its views, the Anthropological Society found it difficult to condemn the brutal slaughter of the aborigines of Queensland and Tasmania going on at that time (Reining 1970, 5). Only later, in 1871, did the two organizations merge to form the Anthropological Society, which now affirmed the unity of humankind.

A second question now arose: if all humans are one species, how can we explain racial differences? The answer, according to anthropologists, lay in biological evolution. All humans belong to one species, but some are more evolved than others. This accounted for their differences, and, not incidentally, justified slavery and colonialism. Europeans had the moral responsibility to help the backward natives become fully human beings. But studies did not support the idea that humans could be divided neatly into different races, such as Caucasoid, Mongoloid, and Negroid; nor did they show the so-called Caucasoids to be phenotypically—that is, in body shape, size, and appearance—further from the apes than Mongoloids and Negroids.

Most missionaries rejected the theory of biological evolution, but they were not immune to the spirit of the time that upheld the superiority of the white race. Stephen Neill writes:

> Missionaries in the nineteenth century had to some extent yielded to the colonial complex. Only western man was man in the full sense of the word; he was wise and good, and members of other races, in so far as they became westernized, might share in this wisdom and goodness. But western man was the leader, and would remain so for a very long time, perhaps forever. (1982, 259)

Unlike Spanish Catholic missionaries who often settled abroad and intermarried with the local people (as in Latin America), Northern European

Protestant missionaries considered their "homes" to be the countries from which they had come. They often lived in compounds segregated from the natives and discouraged the marriage of their children to local people. They looked forward to furloughs and retirement *at home*. This practice protected their sense of superiority.

A second example of racism was the preaching by missionaries in Africa as late as the 1950s that the Africans are under the curse of Ham, and therefore are incapable of ruling themselves. Today we reject this interpretation of Scripture, but as Nzash Lumeya (1988) points out, it is still widespread among African Christians themselves, many of whom believe that Christian institutions will prosper only when a white person is present. In North America, Billy Graham has repeatedly charged that Christians have a sinful accommodation to racism, both in the church and in society. All people have a sense of racial superiority, but whites have had political power and have tried to back it up with science.

Cultural Evolution

When studies of race failed to demonstrate Western superiority, anthropologists turned their attention to cultural diversity. Here the grand unifying theory was cultural evolution. All humans were incorporated into one cosmic story of progress from simple to complex, from savagery to civilization, and from prelogical to logical. The superiority of Western technology and life was self-evident. It enabled the West to conquer and rule the world. It justified the modern Enlightenment view of history.

Unfortunately, for many missionaries the idea of cultural evolution became a part of their *zeitgeist*. It was absorbed with the intellectual air they breathed. Charles Taber notes: "The superiority of Western civilization as the culmination of human development, the attribution of that superiority to the prolonged dominance of Christianity, the duty of Christians to share civilization and the gospel with the benighted heathen—these were the chief intellectual currency of their lives" (1991, 71). The key word here is civilization. During this era the word culture was not used in the way we use it today. So one of the effects was that missionaries viewed the people they served as primitive heathens and attempted to turn them into civilized Christians. Wilbert Shenk writes:

> The seventeenth-century New England Puritan missionaries largely set the course for modern missions. They defined their task as preaching the gospel so that Native Americans would be converted and receive personal

salvation. The model by which they measured their converts was English Puritan civilization. . . . They gathered these new Christians into churches for nurture and discipline and set up programs to transform Christian Indians into English Puritans. (1980, 35)

Most missionaries accepted the superiority of Western civilization, and saw it their task to Civilize and Commercialize as well as Christianize the people they served.[2] They built schools and hospitals alongside churches and saw science as an essential part of the curriculum, nearly as important as the gospel. This equation of the gospel with Western civilization made the gospel unnecessarily foreign in other cultures and linked it to Western rationalism and the politics of American and European nations.

A second effect of the theory of cultural evolution was that missions exported the Enlightenment split between supernatural and natural realities to other parts of the world. Evolutionists argued that prelogical humans invented animism to explain and control their world. Animism is a belief that the world is full of spirits, witchcraft, and magical powers. Anthropologists thought that as humans evolved they developed high, philosophical religions, more logical in character, which displaced animism. Ultimately, humans developed science as a new kind of knowledge based on a new kind of reasoning—positivism, which in time would replace religions.

Missionaries rejected the displacement of religion by science, but they saw these as distinct fields of knowledge. They brought the gospel and planted churches based on theology. But the schools and hospitals they established were generally seen as based on science. Many who studied in mission schools and hospitals rejected the gospel they heard but adopted science. As a result, Lesslie Newbigin (1966) points out, Christian missions has been a great secularizing force in the non-Christian world.

Many missionaries assumed that Christianity would automatically displace animism with its belief in earthly spirits and powers. For the most part, they did not take seriously the people's beliefs in spirit possession, witchcraft, divination, and magic; they simply denied the reality of these. As a result, many of the old beliefs went underground because the missionaries had not seriously dealt with them or provided Christian solutions to the problems they addressed. Today these underground beliefs are resurfacing around the world and creating havoc in young churches, leading to varieties of syncretism and to a split-level Christianity that looks to theology for

2. These tasks came to be known as the three Cs. David Livingstone added Commercialization not with the thought of exploiting the natives but of freeing them. He saw free commerce as the only way to end slavery.

ultimate salvation and to traditional beliefs to solve the everyday problems of life (Hiebert, Shaw, Tiénou 1999).

This supernatural/natural split separated science from religion and gave final authority to the former. As Charles Malik notes, "Science has acquired such overpowering prestige today that according to some people, you cannot hope to get a hearing for what you are talking about unless it is science" (1987, 49). This dualism has led to the secularization of the Western worldview and the weakening of Western churches. Science has come to be accepted as public truth—based on facts and true for everyone. Religions are accepted as private truths—based on faith and true only for the believer. Many Western Christians have turned to religion to deal with eternal matters such as creation, sin, and salvation and to science to explain and control the events of everyday life. Diseases are attributed to germs, and personality problems to psychological disorders. In order to make Christianity credible in societies dominated by secular naturalistic explanations, Christian scholars and schools have increasingly reinterpreted their theologies to fit the modern worldview.

How do we evaluate the effects of the theory of cultural evolution on missions? On the positive side—and there was a positive side—we must remember that the modern mission era witnessed the greatest Christian outreach the world has ever seen. Too often in the West we feel so guilty about the colonial era that we forget that the missionaries, like the explorers, traders, colonial government rulers, and even anthropologists, were people of their times. Moreover, as Lamin Sanneh (1993) points out, missionaries gave the people dignity and empowered them by translating Scripture into their languages. We must retell the stories of the thousands of young people who felt the call of God and went to the ends of the earth, suffering great hardships, and often laying down their lives for the sake of spreading the gospel. Exploration, colonialism, and *pax Britanica* did open the doors for missionaries to serve and plant churches in the most remote corners of the earth. God used imperfect people with imperfect understanding in imperfect conditions to carry out his work in remarkable ways. We who stand in judgment must be willing to make the same sacrifices and realize that we, too, are people of our times and will be judged by those who follow us.

Another positive side of this era was the affirmation of the unity of humanity it provided. In missionary circles there was no doubt that all humans are created in the image of God, are fallen and lost, and are in need of salvation and the opportunity to become followers of Jesus Christ. It was this deep conviction that drove missionaries to give their lives for the salvation of people they did not know. It was this that led them to build schools, hospitals, and agricultural training centers; to call for justice and moral rectitude; to strive to end infanticide, widow burning, and inter-tribal wars; and to identify with the poor and oppressed. Their interest in helping people stood in sharp contrast to the colonial rulers who sought mainly to exploit people and the lands they occupied. In our day we often lack this driving passion, or sacrificial commitment, that turned the world upside-down.

On the negative side, the theory of cultural evolution affirmed Western arrogance, ethnocentrism, racism, and colonialism. It also led to a sepa-ration (even segregation) between missionaries (Westerners) and church leaders (natives). The result was the domination of young churches by Western influences and the inability of young churches to mature into full equals. A hundred years after the founding of the Batak Church in Indonesia, Theodor Mller-Krger wrote:

> So the missionary became the patriarch, who was readily obeyed, and under whose leadership it was confidently believed that all would go well. It is surprising that this position of the missionary was taken for granted and reflected in the order of the Church as this developed. The patriarchal struc-ture of the Church was accepted as the only means by which its stability and its future could be safeguarded. (Neill 1982, 257)

Finally, many missionaries saw little good in the Others' culture on which the church could be built. Every aspect of traditional culture had to be destroyed so that Christianity could be built up according to Western understandings.

The Battle over Humanity

Both missionaries and anthropologists wrestled with questions about the fundamental nature of humans and the realities of human differences. Dur-ing the past century, anthropologists in particular have developed theories to understand the diversity of humans. These have influenced missionary thinking to varying degrees. Like other Western disciplines, these theories have cast light on the understanding of humans, but they, too, are histori-cally and culturally situated and so have their limitations and biases.

One of the critical questions was: what does it mean to be human? Both missionaries and anthropologists had come face-to-face with a bewildering variety of people from different races and cultures, and both had to decide whether they considered these people to be fully human in the same sense that the educated peoples of the West were thought to be human.

The missionaries were committed to the unity of humankind by their theology. Convinced as they were of the truthfulness of their Christian message and its universality, they went to all parts of the world and to every level of society to minister. They considered all humans to be created in the image of God and to have an eternal destiny. But, as anthropologists were all too ready to point out, in public they often depersonalized the people to whom they went.

Some of this depersonalization took place because missionaries were people of their times. Like their contemporaries, they were convinced of the superiority of their culture, and they did not always differentiate this from their faith in the superiority of Christianity. They came from societies that were dazzled by the successes of science and technology and that saw themselves as the end point of an ascending cultural evolution. It is not surprising, therefore, that missions gave little credence to indigenous sciences, social organizations, and religious beliefs. For the most part they were not free of the ethnocentrism of their cultures of origin.

Depersonalization also occurred because Western theology dichotomized the world, including humans, into supernatural and natural realities. Some saw people as spiritual objects to be converted, others as natural beings needing material and social aid. Neither viewed humans from a holistic perspective. To be fair, it must be recognized that at the ground level most missionaries were deeply involved not only with evangelism, but also with relief, education, medicine, development, and social uplift. For example, faced with famine, most did all they could to care for the needy. But the theological dichotomy often led to fragmented programs that ministered to one or another human need but not to integrated programs that served whole peoples. Theologically, the problem was how to deal with people's humanness and its relationship to their divine calling.

Finally, anthropologists charged missionaries with being agents of colonialism. At times missionaries were funded by colonial monies, and they were not above using their relationships with colonial rulers to bring about changes in native cultures, such as ending bride-burning in India and infanticide in other parts of the world. Even more significant was that they shared the basic assumptions that undergirded colonial thought—assumptions that often led to the segregation of Western people mentally and socially from the people they came to serve. When political troubles came, for instance, missionaries might be overly inclined to support colonial powers.

Anthropologists sought to study people in their own contexts and not to change them. This was a matter of being *scientific*. Yet they, too, were guilty of dehumanizing the people they studied. Anthropological dehumanization occurred on the theoretical level. With the general acceptance of an evolutionary approach to human origins, the questions arose: when in the evolutionary sequence did creatures become human, and what sets humans apart from animals? A corollary question was: are all living races of humankind fully human? Debates were held on whether the newly discovered Pygmies of central Africa were humans or apes, and whether tribal peoples had a "primitive mind" that, in some sense, was prelogical and irrational.

Anthropologists also dehumanized people by their attempts to be value-free. Given their growing Rousseauian commitment to the idealization of the lives of "primitives," there was little to justify any applied work in anthropology. Thus rather than help people, they studied them. They adopted the scientific methodology that had worked so well in the physical sciences and sought to give objective, unbiased analyses of non-Western peoples. But "objective" in this context meant detached and value-free. And their detachment dehumanized people by treating them as predetermined objects rather than as rational humans, while their avoidance of values denied help to those in need and those oppressed by the advance of Western civilization. Referring to the Queensland aborigine hunts in which Europeans slaughtered tribesmen of Australia for their land, one anthropologist wrote, "Anthropological science, like all sciences, is passionless on the point, but a better knowledge of its deductions and principles would have instilled some feelings of prudence and piety into the murderers, who seem to revel in the unnatural process of extinction."[3] Still, anthropologists did nothing, for anthropology had little basis on which to build morality or a code of ethics.

Scientific methodology, as it came to be used in anthropology, dehumanized people in yet another way. Given a growing atheistic and deterministic stance, it is not surprising that early anthropologists gave little respect to the people's explanations of their own activities. They treated religions as irrational superstitions and gave scientific explanations for human beliefs and activities in terms of economic and environmental factors on the one hand, and sociopolitical factors on the other. Anthropologists were no less philosophically ethnocentric in their relationship to other cultures and worldviews than were many Christian missionaries.

3. See *Popular Magazine of Anthropology* (1866): 6.

Finally, as Marxist anthropologists in England later pointed out, anthropologists, too, became increasingly involved in colonial processes. The early ones did so by providing an academic rationalization for colonial rule and the "white man's burden"; the later ones did so by providing the field information necessary to implement the move to indirect colonial rule made necessary by budget cutbacks. Even in the period between 1930 and 1950, a great deal of research carried out by leading anthropologists was funded by the British colonial office.[4]

Furthermore, like their missionary contemporaries, anthropologists shared the basic colonial assumption that it was the duty of *civilized* nations to educate and develop the uncivilized ones. Despite the intimate associations they developed with people during their fieldwork, they remained ultimately segregated from the people they studied. Anthropologists also returned to the safety of their academic environments where they could talk as experts about "their people." In the long run, they shared even less identification with the natives than did the missionaries.

Missions and Anthropology: The Late Modern Years

By the 1930s, anthropology had come to accept the basic unity of humankind, but was faced with an apparent unending and arbitrary variety in human behavior and cultural forms. What, then, is the nature of human unity? And how does this variety relate to it? Two movements displaced the theory of cultural evolution in anthropology in the 1920s, both emerging out of close personal encounters with Others in the process of studying them.

Social Anthropology

A new anthropological paradigm emerged after World War I, namely social anthropology, begun in England by A. R. Radcliffe-Brown (1881–1955), Bronislaw Malinowski (1884–1942), and their disciples.[5] Both Radcliffe-

4. This was true of research carried out by Evans-Pritchard, Radcliffe-Brown, and Gluckman, to name a few. Further discussion on this is found in Kuper (1974, 123–49), and in books dealing with anthropology and Marxism.

5. Adam Kuper (1974) traces the history of this school. He notes that it began in 1922, when Malinowski and Radcliffe-Brown published their first major field studies and W. H. R. Rivers, the greatest figure in the prefunctionalist generation, died. Malinowski has a strong claim to being the founder of social anthropology in Britain, for he established its distinctive apprenticeship— intensive fieldwork in an exotic community. The students and students' students produced field

Brown and Malinowski were influenced by the newly emerging science of sociology begun by Emile Durkheim in France. Both did anthropological fieldwork and learned to know Others personally as fully human beings. Social anthropology compared social systems, such as families, clans, tribes, and peasant communities, from around the world and helped us see that social systems are both powerful and functional. It also showed us that humans organize their societies in radically different ways and gave us ways to compare different social systems.

At first, social anthropologists doing fieldwork, such as Sir Edward Evans-Pritchard, sought to give detailed, objective descriptions and explanations of other cultures, but did so using previously established categories and methods of anthropology. These outside analyses viewed human cultures as objects to be studied scientifically. Malinowski went a step further. He argued that to understand Others we must enter their world and see it in their categories. We must be *participants* as well as observers. We must cross the line and identify ourselves primarily with the people rather than the academy. In so doing, Malinowski made us aware of the tension between being a participant and an observer at the same time. We are both insiders and outsiders, natives and scientists, participants who know the native language but also speak English. After Malinowski, in-depth fieldwork became the hallmark of anthropological research.

British social anthropologists studied tribes in various parts of the world, such as Africa and the South Pacific, where lineages, clans, and tribes were living, functioning realities.[6] They showed us that social systems have a life of their own; they are not simply gatherings of individuals. There are deep structures that regulate social behavior. These anthropologists saw each society as wholly sui generis—a unique, bounded, and more or less successful adaptation to a particular environment. Each was made up of parts that function to maintain a harmonious, balanced whole. Each was homogeneous and uniform.

Social anthropology contributed much to our understanding of people, but it had its limitations. It was often reductionist and explained all of the various spheres of human life in terms of social dynamics. For example, cultures and religions were seen as social constructs created to maintain social order. There was nothing ontologically true in them. There was no

---

studies of the various exotic societies over which Britain used to rule and evolved a distinctive mode of analysis from them.

6. Many of the studies were done by British anthropologists in British colonies, often to help British administrators institute indirect rule that worked through local governmental structures.

place for God, spirits, and other supernatural realities. Moreover, societies were seen as morally neutral. There was no place in the theory for oppression, injustice, and human sinfulness. Each society had its own moral norms, all of which served to maintain the society, but for people in one society to judge those in another was seen as ethnocentric and imperialistic. There were no supracultural moral and cognitive universals by which societies could be evaluated.

Early social anthropologists focused their attention on small-scale societies and examined these as closed systems, largely unaffected by outside factors. Consequently, they had difficulties in understanding large, complex societies—such as cities—and global systems. Because of their emphasis on internal functioning, they saw change as invariably bad, and castigated missionaries for changing cultures.

Early social anthropologists saw themselves as objective scientists analyzing humans using scientific categories, methods, and logic. Initially they did not see Others as *humans* to be known personally and intimately. Moreover, they did not account for their own presence in the scenes they described nor did they see themselves and their theories as socially and culturally shaped. What the local people thought about their own societies and cultures was unimportant. What the scientists said about these societies and cultures was the truth. But Malinowski's stress on understanding people from their own point of view was given further definition by the missionary anthropologist Kenneth Pike's distinction between the *emic* (insider, participant) and *etic* (outsider, observer) perspectives. This insight challenged the old belief that scientists are totally objective observers unaffected by their own social and cultural contexts.

Sociology and social anthropology have had a profound impact on Western missions. Early mission strategies were largely based on a geographical division of the world. But missionaries found deep social divisions within the cultures to which they went, divisions that shaped the people's response to the gospel more deeply than geography. This led to the Church Growth movement started by Donald McGavran, Allen Tippett, and Peter Wagner. McGavran and Tippett demonstrated how social dynamics play a major role in the growth and organization of the church. They introduced concepts such as homogeneous groups, people movements, social receptivity/resistance, and social barriers into mission literature. More recent applications of social theory to missions include the People Group movement that defines some seventeen thousand *people groups* and seeks to plant churches in each of them (in part through the Adopt-a-People movement).

There have been benefits from this movement. On the whole, it has assisted us in the task of contextualizing the gospel. For instance, the study of social dynamics has shaped how we view conversion. In the West, we expect individuals to make personal decisions to follow Christ, but in many parts of the world important decisions are made by the significant groups to which people belong—their families, or lineages. In missions, this has led to a great deal of discussion of *mass* or *multi-individual* movements to Christ. Our understanding of church structure has also been influenced. Traditionally, missionaries exported their own home ecclesiologies. Anglicans ordained bishops, Presbyterians appointed presbyteries and synods, and free churches held elections, even if these forms of leadership caused confusion in societies where they were foreign.[7] The questions are: to what extent can local churches draw on their surrounding social systems to organize themselves, and when are they in danger of becoming captive to systems that distort the gospel?

A second benefit has been to enhance our understanding of social distance. Prior to this, missional thinking was based largely on geography. Missionaries went to a country such as India, China, or the countries of Africa. There they divided the countries up between the mission agencies on the basis of comity, and each agency subdivided their territories into mission "fields," with missionaries stationed on each. Missionaries were given responsibility to evangelize a certain number of people. They toured the countryside holding evangelistic services in each village or community. But, as McGavran pointed out, geographic distances are not the only, or even the major, barrier to the proclamation of the gospel. Invisible social walls are very real. People may live a few hundred feet from one another, but socially be a hundred miles apart. We need to understand the dynamics of social distance to understand how churches grow.

A third contribution of Church Growth thinking was to focus the missionary task on planting churches that are socially viable institutions, capable of sustaining and proclaiming the faith. In this, Church Growth is an heir to the legacy of Henry Venn, R. Anderson, and Roland Allen, who stressed planting indigenous churches that are self-supporting, self-governing, and self-propagating. Missions in the past has focused on evangelism

---

7. For example, in rural South India, when elections were introduced in the churches, Christians learned that whoever had the most votes won, so candidates brought their relatives and friends, Christian and non-Christian, to church business meetings. Church politics became village politics. When told that only Christian members of the church could vote, they argued that they did not want to drive non-Christians away by rejecting them. Moreover, these people were all part of their village, the community in which they had to live out their lives.

to the neglect of discipling converts and organizing churches. Today the goal of missions is not simply individual conversions, but the planting of living, reproducing churches and the starting of further church planting movements. In the end, the Church Growth movement has maintained an interest in bringing people to Christ at a time when institutionalization has diverted many missions from their central task.

On the negative side of the Church Growth movement, the emphasis on social dynamics may lead to reductionism. All else may be explained in terms of social dynamics. Understanding and applying social principles are essential to mission outreach, but social reductionism makes it hard for us to account for the work of God in human situations. There is a danger that God, spiritual realities, prayer, divine guidance, and holy living are no longer central to church planting strategies. Moreover, theology may have little significance in shaping the goals and methods of church planting. For example, the question of planting ethnically or class-based *homogeneous unit* churches versus integrated churches is decided largely in terms of growth strategies, not on a strong ecclesiology.

A second limitation of the Church Growth movement is that it runs the risk of reducing church planting to social engineering—if we do the work right, there *must* be positive results. We may be tempted to think that the right formulas will bring about success. Moreover, success may be measured largely in quantitative terms, that is, in terms of numbers of professed converts and viable churches. This is hard to reconcile with the biblical emphasis on faithfulness, holiness, hardship, suffering, and persecution.

A third limitation comes from the early theories of sociology. Initially, social anthropology focused its attention on small societies and examined them as closed systems. Social anthropologists saw societies as harmonious organic wholes. The concept of *people groups* fits best with such a view of small scale societies. But peasant and urban societies cannot be cut up into distinct, bounded people groups without seriously distorting the picture. In large-scale societies, individuals participate in many different groups and cultural frames and do not fully identify with any one of them. Associations, institutions, and networks are the middle level of social organization in urban societies, and macroinstitutions such as nation-states, businesses, and transnational organizations are at the highest level of social systems. Consequently, we cannot really speak of distinct people groups or hope to generate people movements in complex settings.

A fourth weakness of Church Growth is its static view of societies. Societies are depicted as wholes that strive for stasis. There is little place in the model for conflict or change. In mission circles, this has led to calls for conversion with a minimum amount of social change and to an uncritical approach to social systems. People are encouraged to become Christians with a minimum of social dislocation. Social systems are viewed in mechanistic terms and considered essentially good if they maintain social order. They, as systems, cannot be judged as oppressive. Consequently, sin is reduced to personal sins and conversion primarily to inner personal transformation. But societies are not static or completely harmonious. Nor are they invariably good. To argue that they are is to ignore corporate sin and to see the world through the eyes of the dominant parties. All this fits badly with Paul's call for radical social transformation in the lives of new believers and the creation of a new type of covenant community in the church (Rom. 12). The Church Growth approach often produces large but theologically and spiritually shallow churches.[8]

A fifth weakness of this movement is its truncated view of culture. British structural-functionalism and its offspring, including the Church Growth movement, have a strong sense of social organization and the way this plays itself out in the lives of people. But these theories have very weak understandings of culture—of sign systems (such as languages and other sorts of symbols), rituals and myths, belief systems, and worldviews. Moreover, they sidestep theology as central to the missionary task. Consequently they do not deal with the questions of cross-cultural communication, contextualization of the gospel message, and theologizing in different cultural settings. Their focus is on contextualizing the church in local social settings, not the gospel in local cultural contexts. This explains, in part, the limited role theology plays in Church Growth theory.

A sixth weakness is the problem of relativism. British structural functionalism began by viewing other peoples in Western terms. It ended in the 1950s with pragmatism and relativism, which reject all notions of social and cultural evil. In missions, this has sometimes led us to seek to preserve cultures at almost any cost and to avoid judging the corporate sins found in all social systems. In our Western churches, the central nerve of Christian missions is in danger of being cut by the spread of this attitude. Due to uncritical acceptance of the Western worldview, many are no longer certain that Christ is the only way to salvation and that those who reject

---

8. Examples of this are northeast India, Rwanda, and South India, where large people movements have led to large churches, but where corruption, hostility, and killing have continued, little affected by the gospel's power to transform not only lives but also whole societies.

him are lost. Many see missions as cultural imperialism rather than the good news of hope.

Cultural Anthropology

A second theoretical paradigm emerged in American anthropology and came to be known as historical particularism. It was pioneered by Franz Boas (1858–1942), A. L. Kroeber (1876–1960), and their disciples. They studied Native Americans who had been overrun by white settlers, many of whom were forced to live on reservations. American anthropologists could not understand Native Americans without taking history, outside forces, and change into account. Moreover, while the social systems of Native Americans had been radically altered, these people maintained a sense of cultural identity, even in the most difficult and oppressive circumstances. So American anthropologists focused their attention on cultural systems, such as languages, beliefs, myths, rituals, and worldviews. For them questions of continuity and change, and the history of change, were central: How had the Indians survived in the midst of such turmoil when their traditional social systems had been destroyed? Why had some of them acculturated to new ways introduced by Western settlers and others not? Historical particularists rejected the arrogance and ethnocentrism associated with the word *civilization* and replaced it with the word *culture*. This shift in language reflected profound changes in the way anthropologists were beginning to view other peoples. Bernard McGrane writes:

> The emergence of the concept "culture" has made possible the democratization of differences. . . . The twentieth-century concept of "culture" has rescued the non-European Other from the depths of the past and prehistory and reasserted him in the present; he is once again contemporary with us. Twentieth-century "culture" was a concept forged in the teeth of "evolution," in a struggle to the death with "evolution" and the hierarchical scheme implicit in it. (1989, 114)

Anthropologists used the plural form "cultures" to indicate both the variety and the equality of human customs.

Like most scientists of the time, American anthropologists came to the cultures they studied as outsiders, confident that their scientific categories and methods produced objective truth. But, unlike British anthropologists, they focused their attention on cultures as cognitive systems that give meaning to people. For them, cultures are not bounded, tightly integrated wholes. Rather, they spoke of cultural areas, cores, and marginal zones in much the same way linguists were defining linguistic families and regions. Moreover, they saw culture as constantly changing, and change as not invariably evil but potentially good. Consequently, they studied change and supported programs advocating the rights of Native Americans along with human development in general. Overall, American anthropology helped missionaries understand the reality and power of cultural systems, including languages, patterns of behavior, rituals, myths, beliefs, and worldviews.

Cultural anthropologists have helped us to understand the reality and power of cultural systems. This has helped us move beyond literal translations of the Bible to translations that are more sensitive to cultural differences. It has also made us aware of the need to contextualize worship services and rituals, to do local theological reflection, and to engage peoples' worldviews.

DESCRIPTIVE LINGUISTICS

One field that emerged in cultural anthropology was modern descriptive linguistics. As anthropologists studied other peoples, they had to learn oral languages using methods other than those of classical linguistics. The methods of anthropological linguistics have helped missionaries to learn and analyze hundreds of new languages and to better translate the Bible. The American Bible Society team, led by Eugene Nida and including a number of outstanding linguists such as William Smalley, William Reyburn, and Jacob Loewen, contributed greatly to the development of linguistics and translation theory. So, too, did Wycliffe Bible translators such as Kenneth Pike, Dan Shaw, Jon Aarenson, and many others.

These linguistic pioneers developed dynamic-equivalence Bible translations based on a Saussurian view of signs. As we have seen, in classical linguistics, signs (such as words) refer to external realities. The word *tree* points to real trees, the word *water* to real water. According to this view, words are labels attached to objective realities. Different cultures give different labels to those realities, so the translator need only find the locally equivalent words to translate the Bible accurately.

But according to Ferdinand de Saussure (1916), signs do not point to external objective realities but to subjective, culturally created categories in people's minds. The word *tree* evokes an image in the mind of the hearer. Moreover, cultures order their mental worlds differently. In other words, people in different cultures do not live in the same world with different labels attached; they live in radically different conceptual worlds. Consequently, even if there is an external objective reality to signs, it can be known only subjectively.

The positive contributions of these Bible translators cannot be overstated. Their fresh approach to reducing oral languages to writing and to translating and publishing more readable and accurate Bibles has contributed greatly to the growth of the worldwide church. They have also served as pioneer church planters in areas where no other missionaries were serving.

Yet the introduction of dynamic-equivalence Bible translations has raised a number of questions and issues. First, the dyadic view of signs as made up of forms and meanings, and the location of meaning in the minds of people, renders the message totally subjective. In other words, signs and messages are totally human constructs. There is no way to check such meanings against experiences of the external world or objective realities. Consequently, communication is receptor-oriented. It is what hearers hear—not what speakers say—that is the measure of communication. This is a good correction to the sender-oriented communication of the earlier formal translation theory, but it removes any objective criteria for testing truth or the true "equivalence" of the message.

Second, there is a danger of linguistic reductionism. Because communication is so central to human life and to missions, it is easy to use linguistic systems as the model for understanding all human systems. There is a danger of reducing all of culture to communication and to texts to be exegeted. This overlooks the fact that much of culture is not about cognitive meanings that can be explicitly expressed in discursive signs, but about transcendent meanings that can be expressed only through nondiscursive signs. Moreover, culture includes the affective and moral dimensions of life. And all communication takes place in the context of social relationships and systems of power, legitimacy, and economics. Linguists may overlook how communication is most often a means to some end, not an end in itself. Life does not center on how we communicate, or even what we communicate, but on the events in our lives that make up the events of history.

In recent years a new subdiscipline, anthropological linguistics (vs. linguistic anthropology), has emerged that links language to social life. Pioneered by Dell Hymes, Marcel Mauss, Claude Levi-Strauss, Leonard Bloomfield, and others, anthropological linguistics examines how language is used by ordinary people in the many different settings of everyday life. The model here is not of communication as transmission and reception of information, but as transaction and the means to building relationships. In other words, it links linguistic systems to the larger social and cultural systems in which communication is embedded. This field provides valuable insights for missionaries in the communication of the gospel because it analyzes the relationship *between* language and culture. It shows the creative ways that languages are used in building human relationships.

Ethnoscience

Subsequent to Malinowski, many anthropologists began in-depth field research in which they sought to "enter inside the heads" of their informants (cf. Conklin 1955; Frake 1961). The result was ethnoscience, a discipline that seeks to understand and describe the cognitive categories in the culture of a people. It does this by systematically and carefully identifying the semantic fields associated with linguistic concepts. These are then arranged in taxonomies that reflect the organization of those concepts into larger understandings of the world. Several subfields also emerged, including ethnomusicology, ethnobotony, ethnopsychology, and so forth. The advantage over previous ethnographies is that ethnosemantic methods are so precisely defined that studies can be replicated and verified.

Ethnoscientists have been relatively silent about the possibility of cross-cultural comparisons. If the cognitive concepts of a culture are completely described in their own terms, how can cultures be compared? Some ethnoscientists argue that valid comparisons are impossible. One possible answer is to compare the principles of cognition found in different cultures in order to find human universals, a task undertaken by Claude Levi-Strauss and other structural anthropologists (Hnaff 1998).[9] Structuralists argue that the basic functioning of the human brain is the same everywhere, so the deepest elements of cognition, which are evident in institutions from language to social structure, will be the same.

Ethnoscience has contributed much to missiology by providing a systematic methodology for eliciting peoples' cultures and worldviews. The work on ethnotheology by Charles Kraft and on ethnomusicology by Roberta King are examples. But ethnoscience has not succeeded in remaking anthropology. Its first failure is that it has become one of the many streams in the discipline. In part this failure is due to the fact that it has not pro-

---

9. Structuralism here refers to cognitive structure, not the social structures that social anthropologists study.

vided us with a basis for cross-cultural comparisons and for formulating generalizations. In the end, we are in danger of being locked up in different cognitive prisons with no way out or—at best—understanding only one or two other cultures deeply. Any attempts to develop metacultural grids for comparison are accused of destroying the internal integrity of cognitive systems, and even of being ethnocentric. Lamin Sanneh accuses such accusers of being cultural dogmatists (1993).

Second, ethnoscientists, like Saussurian linguists, tend to reduce everything to cognition. There is often a weak view of the affective and moral dimensions of culture and of social systems and their power to shape cultures and persons. There is also a neglect of history as the reality underlying cultures, societies, and persons. Furthermore, the cognitive model is interested only in the subjective aspect of knowledge. There is no accounting for objective truth, feelings that cannot be reduced to words, or morality. But life would be impossible if cultural signs did not correspond in some fundamental ways to the world outside. Hunting game, raising crops, or driving down a road all require that our mental maps correspond at least approximately to the external world in which we live.

Third, in applying ethnoscience to missions there is the danger of letting the context determine the meaning of biblical texts. The meanings of scriptural passages become what people believe them to be, not a communication from outside. Ultimately this leads us to an uncritical contextualization that is willing to bend the gospel to fit each culture and to neglect the prophetic call for all cultures, societies, and people to be transformed by the power of God. This subjectivism, rooted as it is in an instrumentalist epistemology (Hiebert 1999), ultimately leaves us with total cognitive relativism and an inability to determine the truth. Ethnoscience is a corrective to the positivism of early modern anthropology but is in danger of leaving us in a state of mental solipsism.

Symbolic Anthropology and Semiotics

A school of anthropological thought closely related to linguistics is semiotics. This studies the nature of signs such as words, icons, rituals, and other symbols and the way these shape and convey meaning in human cultures. Central to the debate, as in linguistics, are the relationships between forms, meanings, and realities in signs. The answers we give to this question profoundly shape the way we view Bible translation, the contextualization of the gospel in local cultures, and the church in local social systems.

Symbolic anthropologists have made us aware of the power and importance of nondiscursive signs,[10] myths,[11] and rituals in communicating the deep truths, feelings, and morals about reality as these are seen by the people involved (Turner 1967). They show us the importance of sacred symbols and rituals in shaping and maintaining religious beliefs in communities. Given our Western rejection of formal symbols and rituals in our search for individual expression, many of us view symbols and rituals as empty, dead formalism that needs to be destroyed for true inner Christian faith to find expression. But it is we who are impoverished by the lack of nondiscursive signs that speak of the transcendent and the mysterious and cannot be reduced to mere words. This can be seen in how too often we spend our time talking *about* God rather than *to* him. But how do you talk to God? Words alone are so shallow. Communicating with God requires the deeper forms of expression found in symbols and rituals.

Victor Turner and Mary Douglas show that it is difficult to construct and maintain deep sacred beliefs if these are not linked to sacred communities, such as the church, and to sacred rites, such as baptism, the Lord's Supper, birth rites, marriages, and funerals, which give corporate expression to our faith. While retaining our emphasis on personal faith and teaching the truth, we in the West need to learn how to express our faith in church using living sacred symbols and rites that renew and transform us both individually and corporately. This awareness of the role of rituals in religion is particularly important in missions, where we deal with societies in which rituals are central to the people's lives. We of the West are in danger of bringing a gospel that is purely information to be believed rather than a way of life to be lived. So the insights of symbolic anthropology have had great significance for missionaries as they seek to contextualize the gospel in the worship and life of a community of believers.

Another area of symbolic anthropology that impacts missions is the study of worldviews. We have often communicated the gospel in terms of conscious propositions, such as "Christ is the incarnate Son of God who died for our sins, and so on," and surface behavior, such as "don't drink alcohol, attend church regularly, and so on." Too often we are unaware that these beliefs and practices are rooted in deep worldviews that make up what

10. Discursive signs point to realities directly. Nondiscursive signs point to realities that cannot be described by words and other discursive signs, realities including mysteries that transcend description, such as God, love, beauty, and holiness. They evoke the deepest feelings and embody the fundamental values of a culture.

11. The word myth, as it is used here, does not mean fable; used in the technical sense, it refers to the metanarrative by which we understand the cosmic story of reality.

we think *with*, not what we think *about*. This includes the categories and logics we use, the root metaphors and myths that order our understanding of the world, and the fundamental assumptions we make about beauty and morality. Too often we find new Christians talking the right talk without really understanding the Christian worldview. For example, the same prayer can be a supplication to God or a magical formula to make him do our will. There remains much to be done in the study of worldviews and in the study of the biblical worldview (Hiebert 2008).[12]

Anthropology of Religion

Another field in cultural anthropology is the study of religions and religious movements. Early on, the founding fathers of cultural anthropology, such as Tyler, Frazer, and Morgan, recognized the importance of religions as belief systems, but discounted them as prelogical and protological forms of thought. Later, Wilhelm Schmidt and Fritz Graebner of the Vienna School showed that many tribal religions had the concept of a high god who is now distant from humans because of their rebellion against him.[13] As Catholics, they saw these beliefs as bridges for communicating the gospel to these societies.

Evans-Pritchard and other anthropologists began to take religious beliefs seriously and to show that these are not just prelogical fantasies and projections of corporate minds. Robin Horton (1967), Bryan Wilson (1970), and others have done much to help us understand that the logic behind traditional religions is not foreign to us but is rooted in human experience and in universal patterns of thought. In so doing, they have helped remove science from its privileged modern pedestal and see it as one system of beliefs alongside others.

Along another line of inquiry, A. F. C. Wallace (1958) provided us with a framework for understanding religious movements as responses to cultural crises. Building on his insights, Harold Turner (1981) analyzed

12. Some argue that there is no biblical worldview. In a sense they are correct, for there are different worldviews reflected throughout the Old and New Testaments. But if we affirm that underlying all Scripture is a fundamental unity—one gospel—then we need to see how the understanding of God, creation, humans, sin, and other central themes in the Old Testament are sharpened and added to in the New Testament, all toward a better understanding of the unity of God's truth. Our understanding of this will be from our own cultural perspectives, but the global church as a hermeneutical community can help us see our own blind spots and learn to see the deeper truths of divine revelation.

13. Schmidt and Grebner published *Anthropos* and other books seeking to show that the idea of a high god is very old. Evolutionists such as Tylor rejected these claims, but the claims are now widely accepted.

the impact of Christianity on primal religions and the emergence of new emerging religious movements. More recently, Andrew Buckser and Stephen Glazier helped us to understand some of the anthropological dynamics of religious conversion (2003). Much more study is needed to understand the explosion of new religious movements, including locally initiated churches around the world, and the implications they have for Christian missions.

The anthropological study of religion has been helpful to us in missions in terms of understanding other religions. But anthropologists have not raised the most vital question: which of these belief systems is true? It is hard to move beyond phenomenology to ontology—from descriptions of what is observed to statements of what is true. For one, there is the fear of accusations of ethnocentrism and imperialism if such judgments are made. For another, it is difficult to lay foundations for judging between different belief systems, religions, and sciences to determine the truth. We can learn much from the recent studies of religion from the social science perspective. But these do not take spiritual matters seriously, and they fail to point us beyond phenomenology, leaving us by default in a relativistic morass. Yet, as Peter Berger and others have pointed out, at some point we must confront the questions of truth and falsehood, beauty and ugliness, and righteousness and evil, or we are dilettantes and Cretans who watch the world crumble and do nothing about it.

Applied Anthropology

Some American anthropologists, such as Margaret Mead, have focused their studies on culture collision and culture change. They are interested in applying anthropology to social engineering and global development. After some rough beginnings, applied anthropologists are now widely used in government and nongovernment agencies in the fields of social and economic development.

Christian applied anthropologists have contributed to mission programs involving development, such as World Vision and the Mennonite Central Committee. But on the whole, missions have been slow in drawing on the insights provided by applied anthropology. The main danger here is being pulled into a form of social engineering that manipulates people and to a social gospel that forgets the priority of sin and salvation. An example of this is the current interest in "meeting felt needs" in the American church. Yet applied anthropology has much to offer because of its interest in effecting positive forms of change and change agency. Missions would do well to learn some of its lessons.

Fundamental Issues

A number of new issues were raised by anthropologists and missionaries during this late modern period as a result of the development of social and cultural anthropology.

Unity and Diversity

One central issue is: In what way are people one? And how does such a wide variety emerge from an underlying unity? By the 1930s, both missionaries and anthropologists had come to accept the basic unity of humankind, but both were faced with an apparently unending and arbitrary variety of human behavioral patterns and cultural forms.

Missions came to accept this cultural variety. Candidates were taught to face culture shock and to be culturally sensitive to the people among whom they worked. Bible translators had become aware of the fundamental differences among languages and had contributed significantly to linguistic and translation theory. Mission strategists accepted the need for indigenization and contextualization as a matter of course. But this raised other questions: If the gospel and church take many different cultural expressions, then what are the unchanging elements of the faith, and what is cultural and changeable? How should missionaries deal with such phenomena as people movements, polygamy, and homogeneous cultural groups?

Further questions arose out of this debate. One was: how should Christianity relate to the variety of non-Christian religions? Some took the position of radical displacement. Truth was found only in Christianity; therefore, all other religions were categorically rejected and would have to be replaced *in toto*. At the other extreme were those who saw all religions as merely the human search for God, with Christianity nothing more than the closest approximation of the truth. In between lay a multitude of positions stressing, to varying degrees, the uniqueness of Christianity and the presence of truth in other religions.

A second question was: How should the unity of the church manifest itself in the midst of denominational, class, and other differences? Is the church the divine body of Christ, or is it a sociocultural organization subject to the analyses of the social sciences? To emphasize one or the other is to overlook that the church, indeed, is both. But how is it different from the clubs, corporations, clans, castes, and crowds that this world organizes? And to what degree should the church engage in the leadership styles and recruitment techniques of these other institutions?

A third question had to do with the emergence of local theologies around the world: Latin American theologies, African theologies, Japanese theologies, Indian theologies, and so on. If the church in each culture does its own theological reflections, where is the unity of *Christian* theology and where is Truth? In the end, who decides what is legitimately Christian and what is not?

For anthropologists, the questions of unity versus diversity came in another form. Early anthropologists sought to reduce the variety of cultures by incorporating them into a single broad theory of cultural evolution. However, intensive fieldwork made it clear that culture traits such as subsistence technologies, marriage patterns, and religious beliefs could not be understood apart from their particular geographical and historical contexts, and therefore could not be compared with one another. This made it difficult to identify any human universals.

To be sure, there was at the same time some search for cultural universals using the methods of cross-cultural comparison: a search for institutional universals, such as the family; for religious universals, such as the belief in a high god; and so on. But few of these withstood the test of true universality. Each new field-worker found exceptions to any generalizations and discovered still other ways of ordering the world, or yet more fundamental differences among people. The vision of unity faded in the light of cultural variety.

In the face of this variety, and lacking any unifying empirical universals and ethical absolutes, anthropologists turned to cultural relativism. Variety not only was thought to exist at the most basic levels of human thought and behavior but also was extolled as a wonderful human virtue. Even comparisons were called into question. It soon became apparent, however, that pure relativism undermined anthropology's claims to be a universal science of humans and, in the end, to a denial of the validity of science itself.

Humanness

A second major issue facing missions and anthropology at this time was the intrinsic nature of human beings. Despite basic agreement on the unity of humankind, the question of what it *means* to be human was still unanswered.

Missions began to recognize the various dimensions of people—that they are biological, psychological, and sociocultural beings. Cross-cultural training, linguistics, and psychological counseling have since become standard elements of mission training programs, and sociocultural principles and research have become part of mission planning. But this often amounts to a superficial borrowing of a few select concepts that do not disturb the existing theological frameworks.

Missions have yet to develop a theology of culture and society that comes to grips with the issues raised by the social sciences. Some thought has been given to a theology of language (e.g., Ebeling 1973) and social organization.[14] More recently attention has turned to theologies of economics, politics, and power.[15] But these need to be integrated with theologies of ecology, aesthetics, religion, and science to form a broader theology of culture. The underlying question is: how does scientific knowledge integrate with theological knowledge? The two cannot be kept apart, for whether we like it or not, the use of medicine, technology, and other products of science bring with them the assumptions on which science is based. The danger is that these assumptions and their products will be absorbed into theology unwittingly and without critical analysis.

The theological answer to the question of humanness must lie in an understanding of the doctrines of creation and incarnation. If we replace Greek dualism (supernatural and natural) with biblical contingent dualism (Creator and creation), many of the dualisms we see in missions disappear. As John Stott (1979) notes, people are bodies-souls-communities, and ministry to them is not spiritual plus material but rather ministries to whole persons. The doctrine of the incarnation takes into account both the divine and the human dimensions without reducing one to the other and without segregating them. The two are related without the loss of either. The full incarnation is found only in the person of Jesus Christ. But that event can be a fitting analogy for our understanding of humans and the church.

The problem of humanness that anthropologists face is a different one. With no place in their models for the divine nature of humans, they are left with little basis to affirm the dignity and eternal destiny of people. Humans are simply the highest of the animals and have no eternal existence or meaning. Nor do anthropologists have a foundation for determining values and ethics, without which humans are reduced to beasts. Having noted the similarities of humans to lower animals, they are hard pressed

14. Some of the better contributions in this area have been made by Nida, Smalley, Reyburn, Loewen, and others whose writings have been published in the journal *Practical Anthropology*, now called *Missiology*.

15. Pioneering work in this field was done by Jürgen Moltmann, John Howard Yoder, and Orlando Costas.

to define precisely what sets humans apart—and yet they are reluctant to let go of the idea of human uniqueness.

A second problem is inherent in the methodology that the social sciences have borrowed from the natural sciences. This methodology makes a sharp distinction between the observer and the observed and treats the latter as an object that is part of a closed, deterministic system. The observer, on the contrary, is assumed to be rational and undetermined. He or she is therefore in a position to give an objective and unbiased analysis of a situation, based on observation and reasoning, that is assumed to come from beyond the object of study (in this case human behavior). But how can the observer observe without being part of the study?

While this approach has provided many insights into the sociocultural order, it is unable to answer most of the more complex questions facing the social sciences because it fails to take into account that we are dealing with humans who think, feel, and make moral judgments. The growing rejection of the concept of a *prelogical mentality* sprang from the realization that when observers pass judgment on the humanness of others, they are passing judgment on themselves. Human studies are reflexive. Theories that are used to explain others must apply equally to explain the scholar-scientist or humanist.

The theoretical and methodological implications of recognizing the objects of our analysis to be humans are profound. Essentially it means that we must add to the objective basis of knowledge a hermeneutical one. Trying to understand people as humans always involves the process of interpreting their beliefs, feelings, and values from their own points of view.

Implications

Several implications from these studies are becoming clear. First, anthropologists have begun to take the cognitive, affective, and moral dimensions of human beings seriously. Behavioral studies alone are not adequate in explaining human beings. Much remains to be done on developing methods that show us what is going on in other peoples' minds,[16] but the fact that we must take their cognitive systems seriously is now widely accepted in anthropology. Many, in fact, now define key concepts such as culture in purely mental terms.

16. This task has been undertaken by cognitive anthropologists and those working in the field of ethnoscience, as well as by Bateson (1972), Devereux (1967), and others who approach it from the perspective of psychological anthropology.

Together with the recognition of cognitive systems has come an acceptance of the importance of religious beliefs and values. These are no longer
considered meaningless superstitions but charters validating their respective
cultures, and paradigms that help people resolve the paradoxical questions
of life. But much more research needs to be done in the areas of the expressive or aesthetic and the moral dimensions of culture. The Enlightenment
prioritization of cognition and truth needs to be tempered with a serious
study of how different cultures perceive beauty and holiness.

Second, hermeneutical knowledge must be reflexive. As Devereux points
out (1967), major changes take place in the observers during their field
experiences. While most anthropologists would not go so far as Devereux
and hold that these changes in the observer constitute the *real data* for
anthropology, they must monitor their own internal shifts in the encounter
and view these, too, as part of human behavior.

Third, scientific study must take seriously the peoples' explanations
of their own behavior. Moreover, such explanations are "preferable to
causal accounts in all cases—except where the behavior is irrational in
the sense of 'incongruent with accepted beliefs' or where behavior is in
accordance with beliefs that are themselves irrational" (Wiebe 1976, 30).
If this criterion is accepted, anthropology consists of not only rational
explanations from the outside but also hermeneutical explanations from
the inside of culture.

Fourth, as Habermas points out (1971), one of the critical methodological questions becomes that of interpretation. It is impossible to gain a purely
objective analysis of other human beings, for their conceptual world (and
this includes not only cognitive categories, assumptions, and worldviews,
but also memories, feelings, and motivations) must be translated into the
conceptual framework of the observer. In the process of interpretation,
much is lost or distorted. How do we know that we have exegeted the
"text" of culture correctly?

Fifth, the question of ultimate Truth arises. Earlier anthropologists
wrestled with the concept of cultural relativism. Now the discipline is
facing philosophical relativism. To take other thought systems seriously
is to raise the question of their truthfulness vis-à-vis science and the humanities. Anthropology is being forced to confront the problem missions
faced earlier, namely: What is truth and how does one thought system that
claims to be true relate to other thought systems?

Sixth, hermeneutical knowledge must be historical and developmental in
perspective. Unlike natural laws that, generally speaking, belong to steady
state theories, principles associated with life and, in particular, humans,

must take into account developmental changes in the people being studied and in the agents of observation. Cumulatively this leads to fundamental changes taking place in societies and cultures that cannot be explained fully in terms of scientific principles. History is needed.

Finally, human studies call for involvement in the society and lives of the people. One cannot sit dispassionately by when relating to people in deep need. In anthropology, the growing awareness of this has led to an interest in applied anthropology. To be sure, some of this interest rises out of a struggle to survive as a discipline. The limited number of positions for anthropologists in the academy raises the question: anthropology for what? A great many graduating anthropologists are having to find employment outside of teaching.[17] Consequently, there is a growing effort to justify anthropology in American society and to broaden the scope of anthropological participation in the job market.

But interest in applied anthropology runs deeper than this. Today a wide range of activist anthropologists (Christian, Marxist, and others) question whether anthropologists can remain uninvolved in helping Others when they know these Others personally and have the knowledge and power to help them. Does not noninvolvement depersonalize people and preserve oppression and colonialism? This concern is leading to the formation of agencies for applied anthropology and human development and to publicizing efforts by anthropologists who not only study but also help the people among whom they work.

In spite of this increased interest in values and ethics and in the dignity of the person, anthropology has not come to grips with the divine nature of human beings and, therefore, has only partial answers as to what it means to be fully human.

17. For an earlier study of the situation, see D'Andrade, Hammel, Adkins, and McDaniel (1975).

5

Recent Anthropology

In recent years the world, particularly the West, has undergone a profound revolution in its view of reality, human knowledge, and truth. Peter Drucker writes:

> Every few hundred years in Western history there occurs a sharp transformation. We cross what some . . . have called a "divide." Within a few short decades, society rearranges itself—its worldview; its basic values; its social and political structure; its arts; its key institutions. Fifty years later, there is a new world. And the people born then cannot even imagine the world in which their grandparents lived and into which their own parents were born. . . . We are currently living through just such a transformation. (cited in Van Engen 1997, 437)

Postmodernity

In the period following World War II considerable thought was given, both in anthropology and in missions, to the question of the relationship between human knowledge and reality. The new era that emerged is often referred to as postmodernity. In large measure, postmodernity is a reaction to modernity, its arrogance, and its colonial expansion and a concern for the subaltern and oppressed.

Modernity was built on skepticism of traditional knowledge. Postmodernity is built on skepticism of modernity. Earlier, Marx and Engels argued that religions and other ideologies of a society serve the interests of the powerful and that the ideas of the ruling classes are the ruling ideas of a society. Postmodernity argues that science, the central belief system of modernity, is itself an ideology like other ideologies. It has constructed a new sense of rationality—scientific rationality—that destroys earlier rational systems and that serves the interests of academicians who have vested interests in their findings and who accept uncritically the very habits of thinking that need to be examined. Sociologists of knowledge, such as Karl Mannheim and Peter Berger, have shown that science is a product of sociocultural forces and that scientists are influenced by their social and cultural settings. What they observe depends on the interests of their disciplines, their contexts, and their places in society. Moreover, they have their own personal interests in mind.

In the end, as Laudan points out (1977), science is no different from religions or other ideologies. In the end, there is no big picture, no grand narrative, no privileged perspective. All ideologies are constructed by individuals and communities, and none of them can be privileged. Local and marginal narratives must be encouraged and heard.

This skepticism is, in part, the reflexive application of scientific critique to scientists and science itself. Alan Barnard writes:

> Postmodernism constitutes a critique of all "modern" understandings. Postmodernists define what is "modernism" as what is all-encompassing; they reject both grand theory in anthropology and the notion of completeness in ethnographic description. On the latter score, they oppose the presumption of ethnological authority on the part of the anthropologist. Thus reflexivity, and ultimately embodiment, came to the fore. . . . [It] levels its critique at the creation of the "other" (and consequent definition of the "self") as the driving force of all previous positions in the discipline. (2000, 168)

Postmodern anthropologists critique earlier anthropologists for having constructed a metanarrative of Others based on the scientific perspective and the dominance of the West.

Postmodernists such as Derrida, Foucault, and Barthes have attacked structuralists who explained humans in terms of underlying systems, whether social or cultural. The postmodernists stress the importance of history and the unpredictable nature of everyday life, which were suppressed by the abstractions of the structuralist project. They focus their attention not on the structures of society and culture but on the ways people bend and shape these so-called structures in dynamic interaction with one another. For example, they are not interested in the deep structures of languages (*langue*) but in what people say and do in everyday life (*parole*).

Postmodernism breaks down the public-private dualism of modernity and reduces everything to the private sphere. Anthony Giddens, describing the work of Lyotard, writes:

> Post-modernity refers to a shift away from attempts to ground epistemology and from faith in humanly engineered progress. The condition of post-modernity is distinguished by an evaporating of the "grand narrative"—the overarching "story line" by means of which we are placed in history as beings having a definite past and a predictable future. The post-modern outlook sees a plurality of heterogeneous claims to knowledge, in which science does not have a privileged place. (2003, 21)

Thus there are no agreed-upon public truths, only a multiplicity of private ones.

Postmodernists are open in their attack on science, its belief in the unity of experience, and its search for a unified theory of knowledge. Lyotard himself writes:

> We have paid a high enough price for the nostalgia of the whole and the one, for the reconciliation of the concept and the sensible, of the transparent and the communicable experience. . . . The answer is, Let us wage a war on totality; let us be witnesses to the unpresentable; let us activate the differences and save the honor of the name. (1984, 81)

In the end, postmodernity destroys all possibility of agreed-upon knowledge.

If all knowledge is constructed in groups motivated by self-interest, then, as Paul Ricoeur (1981) points out in his hermeneutics of suspicion, we must ask of every ideology what privileges the supporting community gains by insisting on these ideas. Every claim to truth is immediately placed under suspicion. Knowledge no longer becomes an issue of truth, but of power and control. In this sense, postmodernity is a code name for the crisis of confidence in Western conceptual systems, their certainty, and their metanarratives. It is an attempt to demolish the grand structures of modernity.

The response of postmodernity is not to offer a new grand narrative, but to celebrate diversity and multiple stories. All voices must be heard.[1] David Harvey writes:

> I begin with what appears to be the most startling fact about post-modernism: its total acceptance of the ephemerality, fragmentation, discontinuity, and the chaotic. . . . But post-modernism does not try to transcend it, contradict it, or even to define the "eternal and immutable" elements that might lie within it. Post-modernism swims, even wallows, in the fragmentary and the chaotic currents of change as if that is all there is. (1989, 44)

Postmodernity is self-referential, not world-referential. It does not seek to look behind images to a global story. Rather, it is content with the images themselves—with a world of pure surface. It cannot go behind superficial appearances. In literature, texts do not point to authors or things or events. They point to other texts. This intertextuality becomes a ceaseless playful process. Not only does this *deconstructionist* approach argue against coherent plots and perspectives in art and distinctive styles in architecture, but it also argues against any single system of objective truth. All truth, it holds, is perspectival, including science's truth.

Postmodernism stresses the local character of all truth. It is the disintegration of reality—a nonrelational vision of reality. The self, too, collapses. Individuals are no more than ephemeral variables in an eternally repeating machine of identification and rejection. In its attempt to tear down the tyrannies of grand narratives, postmodernity seeks to break down our traditional ways of perceiving form and space. It seeks fragmentation, disorder, and chaos; it affirms eclecticism, fiction, theater, and ephemerality.

Interpretive Anthropology

In anthropology, there have been a variety of responses to postmodernity. As we have seen, with the initiation of ethnographic fieldwork, social and cultural anthropologists worked closely with local people for long periods of time, and they began to take seriously that these were fully human beings who had their own beliefs about the nature of reality and truth. It

---

1. If modernity saw knowledge as a photograph, postmodernity sees it as a collage—a patchwork of many different pictures thrown together somewhat randomly on a page. Levi-Strauss referred to this as bricolage—building a house using the odds and ends of materials at hand.

became important, therefore, for anthropologists to learn how the people they met saw the world around them. This *emic* approach challenged the idea that anthropology and sociology are hard sciences. The key methods shifted from observation to participation and from observable empirical "facts" to hermeneutics—to seeking to understand what is in the minds of the people by examining speech, acts, music, and dance as "texts." Out of this emerged interpretive anthropology, championed by Clifford Geertz and others.

Clifford Geertz (1983; 1988) argues that because anthropology is the study of humans it cannot be reduced to purely scientific observation. Anthropology belongs more to the humanities than the sciences because it seeks to understand what is going on inside people, and that involves the methods of hermeneutics. This is a move away from positivism and objective materialism toward the "communication of lived-through experiences" (Harries-Jones 1985, 234).[2]

Reflexive Anthropology

It should not surprise us that anthropologists who studied abroad began to turn their attention to their own cultures when they returned to the West. Serious ethnographic studies of Western societies and cultures emerged in the mid-twentieth century by scholars such as W. Lloyd Warner,[3] Margaret Mead, David Schneider, and Marshall Sahlins. George E. Marcus and Michael M. J. Fisher (1986) go so far as to say that the primary function of anthropology is culture critique, particularly the critique of Western cultures.

The Christian critique of Western societies and cultures has a long tradition, particularly among those who see the church as a manifestation of the kingdom of God. Now that critique has become part of public discourse (Ellul 1967; 1986; Newbigin 1986). It is not surprising that missionaries who studied the social and cultural contexts in which they served and who identified with sisters and brothers in these contexts used their insights and methods to study their own cultures when they returned home. They began to look at the West not as a sending country but as a mission field and asked the question: how should we respond to it as missionaries? Western Christians assume that they know their own societies and cultures because

2. Epistemologically, this was a shift to instrumentalism. Cf. Hiebert 1999.
3. W. Lloyd Warner did anthropological field studies in Australia, but eventually became known primarily as a sociologist studying class in North American cities.

they live in them. Returning missionaries and non-Western church leaders come as outsiders and are forced to look at Western contexts more deeply from non-Western points of view. Moreover, they have developed theories and methods to do so. It should not surprise us, then, that many of those involved in Western culture critique have been Western missionaries to the non-West and global leaders from around the world.

The task of studying Western social and cultural systems from a missiological perspective has only begun. There are a great many issues that need to be addressed, such as the West's supernatural/natural dualism, mechanistic worldview, radical individualism (Berger, Berger, and Kellner 1973), and myth of progress through redemptive violence (Wink 1992).

Finally, we must ask the critical question: what do non-Western churches have to teach churches in the West? Hugh Montefiore writes:

> Over the last twenty years the Christian mission has made little progress in the west. And yet there has hardly been a period in the long history of Christian mission when the Church at the parochial level has seemed to be better equipped for mission. . . . The position in Western Europe is in stark contrast to that in Africa, where during the last century the Christian mission has registered the greatest advance in all its long history, and also to the position in Eastern Europe or China, where the Church has emerged from a long period of state repression with greater increased energies and vastly increased numbers. (1992, 3)

Reflexive anthropology can assist us to better understand the West and how to contextualize the gospel in it.

Postmodern Anthropology

The study of Western cultures raised the question of the role of the scientist, science, and the Western worldview in the West and in the world. Anthropologists began to study themselves and their own contexts, not only other people. It became clear that anthropology and the sciences are not the detached, objective, disinterested parties they had claimed to be but are deeply involved in shaping knowledge systems that are used in the political, economic, social, and religious activities of different groups of people for their own advantages. So postmodern anthropologists challenge the notion of objectivity, deconstruct metanarratives, and identify the role of power in science.

The study and comparison of Western and non-Western cultures has raised the question of objectivity. For radical postmodern anthropologists, there are no true statements that can be made about another culture. There are only the anthropologist's perceptions and interpretations of parts of a culture (Clifford and Marcus 1986; Marcus and Fisher 1986), or, in the extreme case, what has happened to the anthropologist when he or she was in that culture. As Barnard notes, "Radical reflexivists are happy to write more about themselves doing ethnography than about the ethnographees, their subjects" (2000, 174). The result is a radical epistemological relativism that denies any possibility of knowing—or making known—the truth.

A second theme in postmodern anthropology is deconstruction—the rejection of grand anthropological theoretical truth, along with the notion of completeness, in ethnographic descriptions. For example, James Clifford, in his introduction, attacks the idea of ethnography as a representation of the wholeness of culture and stresses the incompleteness of all ethnographic descriptions (Clifford and Marcus 1986).

A third theme in postmodernity is its interest in power. One of the leaders in examining Western scientists and their theories is Edward Said (1995) in his discourse on "orientalism." He argues that the West constructed a particular depiction of the East, the Orient, that facilitated its domination of the rest of the world by trade and colonialism. Furthermore, the West defined itself as what the East was not in order to legitimize that domination. This raises the suspicion that all grand narratives are merely oppressive ideologies of the elite, including Marxism and Scientism.

Postmodern anthropology raises important questions with which we must wrestle, namely, the ways perspectives shape reality and the ways power is exercised in the definition of reality, both in the community and in the writing and sharing of ethnographies. But there are risks associated with using these questions to deny that any objective statements can be written. Marcus and Fisher write:

> It is possible for this sort of inquiry to slide into simple confessionals of field experience, or into atomistic nihilism where it becomes impossible to generalize from a single ethnographer's experience. The danger in both cases is allowing the anthropologist informant dialogue to become the exclusive or primary interest. (1986, 68)

Postmodern anthropology has its flaws. Ernest Gellner attacks it for its subjectivism, relativism, and self-indulgence. He writes:

> [Postmodernists] agonize so much about their inability to know themselves and the Other, at any level of regress, that they no longer need to trouble

too much about the Other. If everything in the world is fragmented and multiform, nothing really resembles anything else, and no one can know another (or himself), and no one can communicate, what is there to do other than express the anguish engendered by this situation in impenetrable prose? (1992, 45)

Fundamental Issues in Postmodernity

Postmodernity is a radical critique of the limitations and distortions of modernity. This critique has raised deep questions for missions and anthropology. Just as a measure of understanding has been reached on the question of humanness and on cultural diversity and unity, missions are being caught up in a fundamental paradigm shift in epistemology—a change in Western thinking about the nature of knowledge itself that demands a reassessment of science and theology (Hiebert 1999).

Subjectivity of Knowledge

In the nineteenth and twentieth centuries, science was viewed as a process by which the laws of nature were discovered by the systematic use of the human senses and organized into a growing body of knowledge. The scientist was seen as a passive observer who, with proper tools, saw accurately (with a one-to-one correspondence) and without bias an order that existed in nature itself. Scientific statements were the truth because they corresponded to reality. Moreover, they were true for everyone, whether people believed science or not. Science was like a building in which each block of knowledge added to the temple of Truth. In schools and in the general public, the encyclopedia and reference library replaced the Bible as the authoritative source of human knowledge.

In recent years, this concept of knowledge has been challenged as scientists have become increasingly aware that the observer plays a key role in creating knowledge. Einstein pointed out the theoretical implications of the fact that data is gathered from the vantage point of the observer. Whitehead (1938) showed the selective nature of knowledge. Piaget (1966) traced how children develop mental constructs in their attempts to understand and manipulate the external world. Bateson (1972) and Berlin and Kay (1969) showed how the senses themselves impose an order on experience. Freud raised the question of the role of the irrational subconscious in perceptions. Hayakawa (1964) and other linguists pointed out the operation of the mind and language in ordering human experience and thought. Polanyi (1974), Kuhn (1970), and others demonstrated the subjective, paradigmatic nature of knowledge.

Postmodern anthropologists conclude that all cultural knowledge is socially constructed and that all human knowledge, including religions and sciences, are subjective. No longer can Western science claim a privileged position. Science is a way of studying humans alongside other knowledge systems. The result is a complete relativism in epistemology that holds that one can never escape human subjectivity. Ironically, postmodernists seem to make an illogical exception for their own case, that is, for their own evaluation of the full circumstances. Otherwise, their arguments would fall by their own verdict.

Incomprehensibility

A second challenge posed by postmodernity is that the world is incomprehensible. Huston Smith writes:

> Frontier thinkers are no longer sure that reality is ordered and orderly. If it is, they are not sure that man's mind is capable of grasping its order. Combining the two doubts, we can define the Post-Modern Mind as one which, having lost the conviction that reality is personal, has now come to question whether it is ordered in a way that man's reason can lay bare. (1982, 7)

It was science that led us to think of reality as mechanically and impersonally ordered rather than personal. But contemporary science has shattered the cosmology built by seventeenth- to nineteenth-century scientists, leaving us without a replacement. Smith adds, "If modern physics showed us a world at odds with our senses, post-modern physics is showing us one that is at odds with our imagination, where imagination is taken as imagery" (1982, 7). We see a table that appears motionless, but is in fact incredibly *alive* with electrons circling their nuclei a million billion times per second. The chair that feels secure beneath us is actually a near vacuum. Light acts both like a wave and a particle because electrons travel two or more different routes through space concurrently and jump from orbit to orbit without ever being in between. And the whole universe exploded out of a ball no bigger than a pin head. P. W. Bridgman of Harvard writes, "The structure of nature may eventually be such that our processes of thought do not correspond to it sufficiently to permit us to think about it at all. . . . We are confronted with something truly ineffable" (Smith 1982, 8).

Anthropologists are caught in the middle of this paradigm shift. Many still perceive scientific knowledge to be statements of absolute truth. They thereby deify human rationality and the mind. They ignore the fact that there are different systems of reasoning—each equally logical—and that many human decisions are based as much on feelings and values as on reason. Others are aware of the limits of human knowledge. They see all knowledge systems as wholly social constructs. Consequently, there is no way to show that one is truer than another. As postmoderns, they embrace instrumentalism and the epistemological relativity of all human knowledge.

The tensions from this paradigmatic shift in Western thought are beginning to surface in theology as well. There are debates over the nature of theological knowledge and what is meant by the authority of Scripture. In part, these debates have emerged out of how young churches around the world are doing local theologies using their own logic and way of creating categories (Hiebert 1996). But they are also the result of changing epistemologies in the secular world. In any case, the danger in distancing ourselves from positivism is that all our understandings of Scripture are relativized. In radical postmodern thinking, there is no basis for understanding truth (theology) and no way to determine whether what we know is true (epistemology). The result is theological relativism.

Missions can learn from postmodern insights. It is important to be aware that we are social actors within the settings in which we work and that we bring with us theological and theoretical frameworks that are partially culturally constructed. But missions built solely on postmodern foundations would be an oxymoron. First, there would be no gospel that is true for everyone. Second, no one would be permitted to seek to change others. Third, even if someone were to seek to change others, there would be no way to truly communicate with them, because each person is an island to him- or herself. Finally, one would never know if the other, indeed, has understood the gospel and become a follower of Jesus Christ. Theological, scientific, and epistemological relativism destroys the very heart of Christian missions.

Post-Postmodern Anthropologies and Missions

Huston Smith (1982), Larry Laudan (1996), and others have called us to move beyond postmodernity. They see postmodernity as tearing down the arrogance and human centeredness of modernity, but not as building a new, better intellectual home in which we can live. It gives no answers to a world with increasing ecological, political, cultural, and spiritual problems. In modernity, we walked along hard ground, certain of our way. But postmodernity, like a river, challenges us. Either we stop and stay on firm ground, or we venture forward into the river. Once in the river, Peter Berger and Samuel Huntington (2003) note that some are swept downstream. But if we continue to struggle through, we find new firm ground and a way ahead. We need to go beyond postmodernity to post-postmodernity (so far, no widely accepted label has been given to this new paradigm).

Now scholars are turning their attention to the emergence of world systems, including the cultural aspects of globalization: dominant languages, intelligentsia, popular culture, and religious movements (Berger and Huntington 2003; Inda and Rosaldo 2007; Lewellen 2002). Sociology, economics, and political science help us understand global, transnational, and metanational systems. But these macrostudies rarely include the cultural aspect and may overlook local communities and individuals. Both the limitation and the strength of anthropology is that it seeks to understand local people and give voice to the marginals in the world.

Glocal Anthropology

In the past few years anthropologists have also turned their attention to the globalization, localization, and regionalization of the world (Gannon 2007; Herzfeld 2001; Lewellen 2002), inspired in part by Immanuel Wallerstein's idea of a "world system" that links the economies of the smallest societies to the powerful capitalist economies of the West, generally to the benefit of the latter (1974). Thomas Friedman defines globalization as "the inexorable integration of markets, nation-states, and technologies to a degree never witnessed before. . . . This is enabling individuals, corporations and nation-states to reach around the world farther, faster, and cheaper than ever before" (2000, 9).

One central question in the emerging anthropological theory of globalism is the relationship between the global and the local (Cvetkovich and Kellner 1997). Some, like Kahn (1980) and Wolf (1982), have examined the relationship between the global and the local in cultural and economic spheres. Studies show that despite globalization, local and regional identities play crucial roles in the lives of most people. In response to this, the term *glocal* has been introduced to refer to the fact that people live locally, but participate to varying degrees in the emerging global networks of goods, services, and information.

A number of insights emerge from studies of the global-local relationship. For instance, they help us to understand the rise of various fundamentalisms around the world. Many of these are reactions to modernity and globalization and seek to reaffirm traditional identities in the face of the corrosive acids of globalization.[4]

A second insight is that there are different kinds of globalizations that interact in complex ways. Peter Berger and Samuel Huntington (2003) list four major globalizing forces: (1) the spread of the English language; (2) the globalization of Western intelligentsia; (3) the rise of global popular culture propagated by businesses such as McDonald's, Disney, and MTV; and (4) popular movements such as environmentalism, feminism, and above all, evangelical Protestantism, especially in its Pentecostal version. While many cultures contribute to globalization, the dominant one now is American in origin and content.

The glocalization of the world and church has profound implications for missions in the twenty-first century, implications we have only begun to explore under the topics of truth, contextualization, ecumenism, partnership, local and global theologies, and religious pluralism. It is important to note that, as Brian Stanley points out, "The missionary movement has been portrayed as one of the earliest forces of 'globalization,' creating networks and new media of communication no less powerful than those established by the global market and information technology of the twentieth century" (2001, 1). This was true of Catholic missions in the sixteenth and seventeenth centuries, and even more so of Protestant missions in the eighteenth, nineteenth, and twentieth centuries. So the issues we face are not new, but they are taking on an urgency that we have not faced before.

How should churches around the world relate to one another when there are great social, cultural, and theological differences, despite a commitment to the truth of the gospel and to the equality and dignity of all churches and individuals, along with their right to participate in the global processes? What does partnership mean when it comes to finances, confessions of faith, evangelism, and mission?

First, underlying the questions raised by glocalization for Christians is the question of the nature of the universal church: should globalization in the churches be developed from the top down—from centralized institu-

---

4. A. F. C. Wallace's analysis of revitalization movements as reactions to modernity can help us understand fundamentalist and other religious and political movements.

tions built around specialists—or should it be developed from the bottom up, beginning at the local level and developing dialogues, partnerships, and global networks of fellowship and ministry? If the latter, then on the theological level we need a metatheology, an agreement on how we do theology (Hiebert 1994).

The globalization of the church also raises questions regarding the role of missionaries. In the past, the missionary went from the "Christian" West to the "pagan" non-West. Today there are large churches and mission movements in non-Western countries. There remain many areas where there is little Christian witness and a need for missionaries. But all missionaries now have a new role as *inbetweeners*. They are bridge-persons, culture brokers, who stand between worlds and help each to understand the other. They stand between the church and unreached peoples and between churches and missions in different lands. This calls for a new understanding of the psychological, social, and cultural nature of the missionaries of the future. They must truly be *bicultural* or *transcultural* people, living in different worlds but not fully at home in any of them.

A second insight from glocalization studies has to do with methods. In mission, we too often use the methods used in the past, which are based on small-scale, tightly knit, resident communities. Then we wonder why we are not effective. In the modern world, people no longer belong to people groups. They participate in many different intersecting communities and do so in different ways. The assumption that we can foster "people movements" in complex urban settings needs to be reexamined. We need to develop an ecclesiology and missiology that enables us to bear bold witness in a glocal world with its global powers, regional loyalties, and local identities.

A third set of insights emerging out of the anthropology of glocalization has to do with migrants, immigrants, and refugees, both forced and voluntary, legal and illegal. Today an estimated 100 million people live outside their countries of original citizenship (Lewellen 2002, 123). Regarding refugees, Lewellyn writes, "The 20th century might deservedly be called the Age of Refugees; it is estimated that there have been 140 million people uprooted by war and the threat of political violence this century. In 1994 alone, there were 23 million refugees" (2002, 171).

Most immigrations take place through networks of kinship and friendship. This has important implications for outreach to a growing population of displaced peoples in the world. Many immigrants and refugees, particularly those who have migrated to the United States, are very open to the gospel extended to them through hospitality. More research needs to be done on immigrants and refugees and on how they can be reached with the Gospel through friendship.

Closely related to immigrations are diasporas—people who share a collective identity and who are spread around the world but maintain networks that sustain and nurture their common beliefs and practices. Examples are the Jewish, Chinese, Sikh, and Armenian diasporas (Cohen 1997). They raise the question of what is "local." The old definition referred to space—a particular place and small size. But in a globalized world, it makes more sense to define "local" in relational and contextual terms (Appadurai 1996). The "local" has been deterritorialized. It is something people carry with them. We can speak not only of local neighborhoods, which are self-reproducing *life-worlds* of relatively stable associations and shared histories, but also of transnational communities and *virtual neighborhoods* (Lewellen 2002, 187–201).

Another type of immigrant, then, is the transnational. A transnational is a person who maintains active, ongoing connections in both home and host countries and often with communities in other countries as well. Transnationalism is growing due to cheap, rapid travel, instantaneous communication, and the internationalization of corporations and job markets. Transnationalism leads to new hybrid identities that connect international communities (Crush and McDonald 2000).

A fourth insight provided by glocalization theory is that identities in the modern world are constantly constructed and contested. In small communities, identities are often ascribed according to birth. On the regional and global level today, identities are created and mobilized for political and economic reasons, often as a means to defend one's self and one's own people, or to subjugate and control others. This has particular significance for the creation of Christian identity in a global world (Huntington 1996).

Advocacy Anthropology

Early on, Marxist anthropology stressed the role of grand narratives, or ideologies, in promoting the evils of oppression and exploitation in human social systems. It emphasized the need to transform not only individuals but also whole social systems by challenging "false consciousness." Its solution was revolution and the replacement of old social systems with new ones, by violence if need be. But it could not guarantee that the new social order would be any less repressive than the old. It had no place for God and spiritual realities, nor for personal and community redemption.

At the end of the twentieth century, anthropologists such as Peter Harries-Jones (1985, 224–48) challenged the very assumptions of the mid-twentieth-century approach to the study of humans and provided a new direction for anthropology in the twenty-first century. Jacob Loewen writes:

> Harries-Jones observes that in the past anthropologists who enjoyed the hospitality of a people over a period of months or years usually wrote an ethnography as a return "gift." They wrote it, however, in the language and intellectual categories of the researcher's culture, not of the host culture. These researchers "piously" hoped for a "trickle-down" effect. That is, as more Westerners learned more about these exotic peoples, benefits from the academic industrialized world would trickle down to the former host society. This, says Harries-Jones, never happened! In fact, the anthropologists' work often exposed these societies to exploitation by the Western industrialized world. (1992, 42)

Harries-Jones notes that anthropological research is based on the assumption of an exchange of communication between human equals of two different cultures. In fact, anthropologists saw the local people mainly as informants and objects to be studied, "as a mine whose product was extracted for export to the Western academic community" (Harries-Jones 1985, 227; Loewen 1992, 47). Rarely is there a genuine two-way exchange of information in ethnographic research. Moreover, ethnographic studies carry no commitment of responsibility on the part of the anthropologist to the community in which he or she has lived and studied.

Harries-Jones and others (Anderson 1985, 45–48; Maybury-Lewis 1985, 136–48) point out that the day of moral neutrality is over. Knowledge produced by anthropologists is used both by the participants of a culture and by others, in the social, economic, and political arenas of life. In the past, anthropologists have interpreted others from the point of view of Western culture. Today they must also interpret from the point of view of local peoples to those in power. Harries-Jones argues that anthropology can no longer be taught as an objective, morally neutral description of culture. "Cultural knowledge carries with it responsibilities to facilitate mutually beneficial interaction between different social and racial groups" (Loewen 1992, 48). Consequently, anthropologists must be advocates helping minority communities cope with the impact of majority cultures in a rapidly changing world (Anderson 1985, 225).

Jacob Loewen notes that, on the whole, missionaries have been less guilty than anthropologists of exploiting the societies they studied (1992,

48). They have stayed longer and sought to serve the people they learned to know more. However, both parties, missionaries and anthropologists, have sometimes collaborated with governments—and other outside agencies—and even now many see ethnographic knowledge not as a way to build deep mutual relationships but as useful tools to carry out their own agendas more efficiently. In missions we must be careful that the knowledge we have is used to the benefit of the people we serve and not to their detriment.

Fundamental Issues in Post-Postmodernity

A number of key issues are central to the emergence of post-postmodernity. These affect not only anthropology and the sciences but also our understanding of Christianity and missions.

Epistemology

Postmodernity is essentially a crisis in epistemology. Postmodernity undermines the positivist epistemology of modernity, but is left with an instrumentalist relativism that has no place for absolute truth. The epistemological foundation for post-postmodernity is critical realism (Barbour 1974; Laudan 1996; Hiebert 1999). In this we reaffirm the fact of an objective reality that can be truly known. We may not see everything, and what we see may be seen as through a glass darkly. But we *do see* enough to become and live as humans. A critical realist epistemology gives us a way to move beyond the postmodern critique, which has been an important corrective but has no solution to offer us in our human dilemmas. The critical realist approach takes us to a post-postmodern worldview.

In this critical realist epistemology, knowledge is not like photographs of reality but like maps or models of reality. But if knowledge is like a mental map, it is not composed of absolute statements of reality, rather of approximations of it. It does not literally correspond one-to-one with reality. We cannot speak of it as ultimately "true" or "false" in the old sense of these terms. The tests of a good map or model are its fit (the degree to which it conforms to our experiences regarding what it claims to be true), usefulness (how it helps us to achieve what we set out to achieve), inclusiveness, uniformity, simplicity, aesthetic beauty, and balance. Maps never give us the total picture—reality is infinitely greater than our knowledge of it. Because they are approximations, maps are subject to additions, change, and improvement as new knowledge is gained. Although maps are not absolute and complete statements of truth, this does not mean that they are arbitrary. "Approximate" must be sharply differentiated from "relative." Maps can fit or reflect accurately a real world, a given, or an absolute on what they claim to be true.

For Christians, the shift to a post-postmodern epistemology should be most welcome because it brings us closer to the biblical perspective on the limits of human knowledge and the importance of faith in knowing. Moreover, it restores affective and moral dimensions to cognitive ones, and relational elements to the very concept of "knowing."[5] And this can help us in dealing with the relationship between local theologies, including Western theologies, and theology as universal truth. In missions it provides a more adequate basis for Christian witness to non-Christians and for the unity of the international church despite cultural and theological differences.

The semiotic shift that is a part of this epistemological shift is a move from Saussurian linguistics to a modified reference theory of signs. It affirms that we can, in fact, speak about truth. Formal linguistics saw signs as referring directly to objective realities. And Saussure argued that signs are merely tied to images in human minds. But a postcritical approach to semiotics is provided by Charles S. Peirce (1958), who pointed out the triadic nature of signs; that is, that signs are culturally formed symbols that point *both* to objective or external realities and to subjective mental images. Signs, then, link the external world to the internal world. Because we all live in the same external world, we can learn to understand how different people see it, and test between their perceptions to determine truth.

According to Peirce, signs vary in the way that they are linked to realities. In the case of idols, the form is the reality—there is no sign at all because the rock image is the god. In the case of icons, the link is still very close but goes beyond surface appearances—the cross for Eastern Orthodox Christians is not the literal cross of Christ, nor is it merely a reminder of Christ's death. It is a powerful symbol that points beyond itself to the mysteries of the reality of Christ's sacrifice that cannot be reduced to mere words and that evokes not only profound truths but also deep feelings and volitional responses on the part of the true worshiper. In the case of ordinary signs such as most words and symbols, the link is arbitrary and discursive. Communication in Peircian terms is measured

5. In Scripture, to "know" takes on different meanings. Sometimes it is "to know about" something. This kind of knowing is at the heart of science. Sometimes it is a far deeper, more intimate, relational knowing, as in the case of the marriage of Adam and Eve (Gen. 4:1). It is this kind of knowledge that interpretive anthropology seeks to understand—namely, intimate knowledge of another, not simply knowledge about them.

by the correspondence between what the speaker says and what the hearer understands. This can be determined, in part, by checking both perceptions with the external realities to which they refer.

Brent Berlin and Paul Kay's cross-cultural studies on color (1969), Eugene Hunn's (1982) study on taxonomies of birds, and Jay Miller's (1982) study on cognitive categories have shown that some cultures lump together certain species that other cultures split apart, but there is a basic agreement on the fundamental categories of nature. In this they confirm Peirce's view that signs link the inner, mental worlds of people to their external worlds. It is increasingly clear that part of the order we perceive in knowledge exists in the external world, part is imposed by the senses, and part is created by the mind. Thus knowledge is not like photographs of reality but like maps or models of it (Hiebert 1999).

Cosmic Narrative

Postmodernity challenges all metanarratives. In so doing, however, it leaves humans with no sense of meaning and place. Huston Smith notes, "I have tried to spell out my reasons for thinking that comprehensive vision, an overview of some sort, remains a human requirement; reflective creatures cannot retain the sense of direction life requires without it" (1982, 16). We find meaning in being part of something much bigger than ourselves—something that is eternal. For Christians this is the cosmic story of God and his mission in creating the universe, redeeming it, and establishing his kingdom.

Missions in the Twenty-first Century

The emerging post-postmodern understanding of knowledge and reality have profound implications for missions and evangelism. In response to modernity's claim that science is public truth and religion is private beliefs, and to postmodernity's claim that there is no truth, only cultural perspectives, Lesslie Newbigin challenges Christians to reaffirm Christian truth as public truth—true for all whether they agree to it or not. In a sense, Newbigin's is a post-postmodern response (Smith 1982). He does not argue that we can "prove" the gospel to be true using empirical methods of modern science. Nor should we be content to affirm our beliefs but allow all other claims to be true as well. We can bear bold witness to what we believe, not based on subjective experience alone but on our right to make truth claims that derive from that experience and from our own particular stance. As E. S. Jones noted, we are not God's lawyers but his witnesses, bearing testimony to what we believe to be true. As we have seen, Newbigin's challenge has led to the Gospel in Our Culture movement both in England (Montefiore 1992) and in the United States (Hunsberger and Van Gelder 1996).

To review: how can we communicate the gospel to other cultures when we live in our own particular human contexts? We need to study Scripture to understand and to bear witness to the gospel. But studying Scripture alone does not help us to see our sociocultural biases, and it often leads to a failure in missions to communicate the gospel in a way that people understand and believe. We need to study humans to understand ourselves and others and to communicate accurately. But studying humans alone has led to relativism and leaves us with no gospel to share. We need both—to study divine revelation and human contexts—and we need to communicate that revelation in ways that remain true to it and yet are understood by people. Failure to do so leads to syncretisms in which the truth of the gospel is lost and the people go astray.

In many ways anthropology and missions are like half-siblings who share—at least in part—a common parentage, are raised in the same settings, quarrel over the same space, and argue the same issues. It is unfortunate that this has often led to polarization and mutual hostility, for each has much to learn from the other. With the growing awareness among anthropologists that they must face the overwhelming problems of a real world (problems that missionaries have faced for a long time), and among missionaries that they must deal with people in their sociocultural contexts (something anthropologists have understood well), a greater mutual understanding and exchange of ideas seems possible.

6

A Systems Approach

As we have seen, to do missional theology we must study humans and their contexts. Anthropologists have given great attention to this and provide us with deep insights into how to do so. So have biologists, psychologists, doctors, historians, and theologians. How do we integrate their findings to get the whole picture of what it means to be human?

Furthermore, we have seen that there are two main types of analysis that have emerged: synchronic and diachronic. The former looks at the structure of reality in a slice of time. It examines the parts and how these relate to one another and to the whole. Its strength is that it sees the underlying structure of human beings (that which is common to us all) and notes how this structure operates to make life possible. Synchronic studies have their limitations. They must put aside the fact that humans live in time and are constantly changing. They present their theories as historical universals that apply to all people. These theories also tend to be highly abstract and hard to apply to the particularities of everyday life. Many are helicopter views of humans, seeing people in general terms, overlooking the uniqueness of each individual. Moreover, with specialization, these disciplines are separated into different research traditions with little attempt to develop an integrated theory that draws insights from them all.

The second type of study of humans is diachronic. Here, time is the central variable. The focus is on the story of each individual, community, and nation and how these fit into one comprehensive human history. The strength here is that we see humans as real people with all their particularities and idiosyncracies, and we hear the stories that give meaning to their lives. The weakness of this type of study is that the structures identified by synchronic studies are out of focus, and general principles may be lost in the confusion of facts on the ground.

Both synchronic and diachronic analyses are necessary to understand humans. These are not competing perspectives. They are complementary. But when one is in focus, the other is out of focus. It is difficult, therefore, to keep both in mind even as we look through the lenses of one or another of the research traditions. In this chapter we examine the synchronic approach to the study of humans. What are the components, and how are these organized into larger structures and systems? We must also study humans diachronically—as beings that change over time in human history. For this, we can call on missiologists trained in history or social process.

Integrating Multiple Perspectives

Various attempts have been made to integrate the insights from the different social sciences. Each attempt has implications for the way we view humans and their humanness.

Reductionism

The simplest way to integrate different perspectives is through reductionism. Here all insights are noted but ultimately reduced to a single explanatory system. Religious truths are reduced to cultural beliefs, cultural beliefs to social constructs, societies to aggregates of individual humans, humans to animals, animals to chemical reactions, chemical reactions to atomic particles, and atomic particles to quantum particles. In the end, there is nothing but masses of vibrating strings. All the rest, including humans, is epiphenomenal.

This way of integrating knowledge is self-defeating. About physical reductionism Ludwig von Bertalanffy writes: "Regarding this theory, I am in fundamental disagreement, not because of . . . metaphysical prejudices, but because the theory does not fit the facts. . . . Human beings (and organisms in general) are not stimulus-response machines, as the theory presupposes" (1981, 15). Logically, if reductionism is applied to scientists, who are humans, even they and their theories are nothing more than strings vibrating in different patterns.

One particularly devastating form of reductionism is scientific reductionism (fig. 6.1). This is common among scientists who are functioning atheists or agnostics and therefore reject the claims of religion. Some see religion as a useful fiction that holds societies together. Others see it as a harmful opiate that justifies oppressive social systems. In any case, these scientists see religion as a human creation having little to do with truth claims. Few Christians would consciously admit to embracing scientific reductionism. It is, however, one of the fundamental assumptions on which most scientific theories are built. An uncritical use of these theories leaves the supernatural outside our everyday lives and undermines our faith in God.

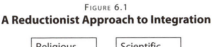

FIGURE 6.1
A Reductionist Approach to Integration

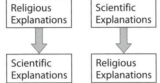

A second form of reductionism is spiritual reductionism. Some Christians reject scientific knowledge altogether. They attribute all human problems, such as illnesses, to spiritual causes and refuse to go to science for answers for fear that science will lead them astray. Others are willing to make use of scientific knowledge because it is useful, but do not seriously examine the conceptual foundations on which it is built.

There is a real danger that we as Christians living in science-saturated, modern societies will live bifurcated lives, functioning with a measure of mental dishonesty. On one hand, most of us are willing to use what the sciences have to offer—modern medicine, cars, television, airplanes, computers, cell phones, communication theories, counseling insights, and knowledge of human societies. On the other hand, we are unwilling to give credit where it is due for these advances in human knowledge and technology. More seriously, in using the ideas and the products of the sciences for practical purposes, we bring its assumptions into our thinking unawares. It is not uncommon, for example, to find Christians who express faith in Scripture but who live their lives on the basis of pragmatism and materialism.

Stratification

A second way to integrate different perspectives on humans is compartmentalization—what Clifford Geertz calls the "stratigraphic method" (1973, 37). The validity of each discipline is accepted, but each is assigned to a different layer of understanding (fig. 6.2). Physical realities are studied by physicists, biological realities by biologists, psychological realities by psychologists, social realities by sociologists, and cultural realities by cultural anthropologists. Little serious attention is given in the secular academy to integrating these into a comprehensive picture of humans, and essentially no attention is given to spiritual realities.

Figure 6.2
A Stratigraphic Approach to the Study of Humans

The stratigraphic approach leads to a sharp division between science and religion. Science studies the natural world using empirical methods; religion studies the supernatural world using dogma and faith. Some theologians, such as Friedrich Schleiermacher, argue that the sciences are matters of fact and truth. Religion, they say, is a matter of feelings—it provides people with meaningful transcendent experiences. Some philosophers, such as Immanuel Kant, argue that religion is a matter of morality—it provides people with values that regulate their behavior and make corporate life possible. Most believing Christians reject these views. Christianity, they hold, is about facts and truth as well as morality and experience.

Modernity imposes another stratigraphic dualism on us. As Lesslie Newbigin points out (1989), in the West science is seen as public truth. All students, including those in Christian schools, must study mathematics, physics, chemistry, and the social sciences—they are matters that are true for everyone. Religion is seen as a matter of personal truth, which can be taught only at home, at church, or in private schools. No classes on Christianity, Islam, or Hinduism can be taught *as truth* in public schools. They can be studied only as human phenomena. While this compartmentalization enables people of different religions to live together, it undermines their convictions that their beliefs are part of the greater Truth. Christian "beliefs" are left to govern Christians at home, but scientific "truth" rules their public lives (Bellah et al. 1985).

Compartmentalization in a more subtle form finds wide acceptance in Christian circles. Many Christians affirm Christian truth with regard to the gospel and supernatural matters such as sin, salvation, miracles, and prophecies, but they use scientific theories to deal with "natural events" such as illnesses, technology, and business decisions. This leads to an otherworldly Christianity and to the secularization of everyday life. It also produces a sharp distinction between evangelism, which is seen as a spiritual matter, and social ministries such as medicine and education, which are left to the sciences. A recent variation of this dualism is to use theology to define the gospel, but to use the methods of social and business sciences to grow churches. This approach fits the American worldview with its emphasis on human control, planning, pragmatism, problem solving, and *doing something*.

Reducing Christianity to emotions, values, private opinions, or supernatural truth secularizes large areas of our lives. If we preach Christ but turn only to secular sciences for answers to our everyday problems, we fail to become his true disciples. We are busy planning and working, but paying little attention to God himself and what *he* wants us to be doing. Scripture is clear: God created both the heavens and the earth, including humans, and he continues to be constantly involved with both.

Integration

A third approach to bringing together different perspectives in the study of humans is to integrate them into a single metatheory. Ideally, we would like a grand unifying theory that incorporates all knowledge into one system of explanation. In reality, this is impossible to do fully because we are finite humans and cannot comprehend at one time the enormous complexity of reality. At best, our theories are always partial explanations. It is also true that we live in human cultures that shape how we think and live. As humans, we cannot occupy a position outside societies and cultures. Even our attempts to develop metacultural grids are themselves formulated in the symbols and thought patterns of particular cultures (for instance, in languages).

Furthermore, to bring different perspectives together, we must recognize that each research tradition focuses on certain aspects of human beings, and, of necessity, leaves out many others. The analogy of maps helps us understand the nature of human knowledge. To fully understand a city, for instance, we need a number of maps, each of which tells us part of the truth. We need maps of roads, political jurisdictions, sewage and electrical systems, building zones, and so on. It is impossible to chart all the facts about a city on one map. Similarly, to describe human realities we need different theories, including theories from theology, anthropology, sociology, psychology, biology, chemistry, and physics.

Each contributes to our understanding of the whole. None is complete in and of itself.

Nonetheless, especially as Christians, we do search for a larger understanding that will incorporate the smaller understandings of the different disciplines. For this, a useful analogy is blueprints. To construct a house, we need different blueprints diagramming different parts of the building: structure, wiring, plumbing, and landscaping. But in this case there does exist one master blueprint that represents the overall structure of the house. As Christians we hold that this encompassing "blueprint" for understanding humans is a biblical worldview. That worldview helps us to see the big picture of reality. The biblical blueprint begins with the God of the Bible and includes the reality of an orderly creation, humans shaped in the image of God, the fall, redemption through the death and resurrection of Christ, and eternal life in him. The fullest expression of this worldview is found in the New Testament and in the teachings of Jesus.

Theology, science, and the humanities chart the details and applications of this worldview. When they conflict, we must reexamine both our different understandings and our worldview to seek a resolution. To continue the analogy of blueprints, the various blueprints of the same house must be complementary, that is, the information they provide must fit together without contradiction. For example, the electrical blueprint should not show wires running where the structural blueprint shows no wall. In complementarity, then, we take the theories of each discipline seriously with regard to its own context, the questions it asks, the data it collects, and the methods it legitimates. But we must also check to see that it is congruent with theories from other disciplines. And we must seek to integrate the findings of each discipline into a larger picture.

Systems

In recent years, the systems approach has emerged as a powerful model for studying complex realities. The pioneer was Ludwig von Bertalanffy (1981). Since his work, the concept has undergone elaboration and critique, and now provides a well-developed theory of complex organizations. Systems theory is now used to understand such complex fields as ecology, psychology, biological life, the military, and institutional organizations.

What is a system? Howard Brody and David Sobel give us a starting definition:

> A system is an organized set of components that is conveniently regarded as a whole consisting of interdependent parts. The parts can be replaced by

similar parts without severely disrupting the system, but the alternative of the organization among the parts will disrupt the system. Each system can be a part of another higher-level system. A hierarchical pattern of system of systems can be formed to represent living systems. Parts of a system are organized and function under the influence of the information flow in the systems. The information flow often takes the form of feedback loops. There are basically two kinds of feedback: a negative feedback to return the system to previous equilibrium and a positive feedback to stimulate growth and maturation. Each level of hierarchy has its specific information patterns. The information flow is not limited to a hierarchical level. It may influence the adjacent levels and even jump to influence widely spaced levels. (1979, 3)

Systems approaches to integration see causality as multidirectional. Both reductionist and stratigraphic approaches are based on linear logic. A causes B, which in turn causes C. To integrate different parts without reductionism or a stratigraphic view we need a systems view of causality. A can cause B and C, but B and C can also cause A (fig. 6.3). The three are related, and change can start in any one of them, affecting the other two. Von Bertalanffy writes: "You cannot sum up the behavior of the whole from the isolated parts, and you have to take into account the relations between the various subordinated systems and the systems which are super-ordinated to them in order to understand the behavior of the parts" (1981, 68).

FIGURE 6.3
Linear and Systems Causality

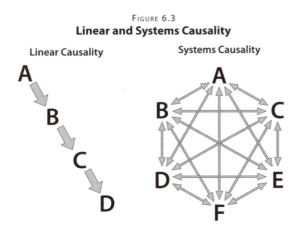

Thus in systems, no one variable is the underlying cause for change. Social changes can lead to cultural, psychological, and biological changes. But changes originating in culture will bring about changes in social organization, personality types, and material culture. Similarly, spiritual transformations will affect social, cultural, and other dimensions of human life. And, there are feedback loops in which changes in one variable cause changes in other variables that, in turn, affect the original variable.

Also, in systems the whole is greater than and different from the sum of its parts. This means that single components cannot be properly understood apart from their place in the overall system. And complex systems must be understood in terms of the ways that parts and subsystems function, particularly the way that they continually change their relationship to one another and to the system as a whole—and, in fact, to the environment around them. In the end, all living things and all their subsystems are spontaneously active.

Finally, systems are frequently structured such that individual parts are themselves systems at the next lower level. The result is a hierarchy of structures that combines systems into ever higher levels of order. At the highest level we have what some call a "system of systems."

Mechanistic and Organic Systems

Systems can be divided into two broad types: mechanistic and organic. Examples of mechanistic systems are clocks, trains, cars, and computers. These are closed systems based on the notion of equilibrium. For mechanistic systems, disequilibrium reflects a breakdown in order due to disruption by external forces (fig. 6.4).[1]

Organic systems are open systems. Examples are living beings such as cells, organs (liver, heart), and organisms (plants, animals, humans). These also include larger systems of organisms, such as ant colonies and bee hives. In human systems, these include groups, organizations, societies, and, ultimately, the global human web. We will focus here only on living human systems.

Living systems share several characteristics. First, in contrast to mechanical systems that are static and in which systemic changes are signs of malfunction, organic systems are in constant disequilibrium and change. No living system is stable for long. Changes may be good or bad, but equilibrium is a form of death. This quality of change is remarkably similar among an unexpected array of systems ranging from simple cells to humans, corporations, nation-states, global systems, and the earth. The contrast between mechanistic and organic systems can be seen by way of illustration. Airplanes are flying machines. In flight their wings do not move. Birds are

---

1. Talcott Parsons, Edward Shils, and other leading human scientists used a general systems approach in their studies of people. But like the early social and cultural anthropologists, they used a mechanistic approach to systems, which led them to see social and cultural systems as harmonious and static. This weakness should not lead us to a rejection of a system-of-systems approach but rather to looking at humans in terms of organic systems—systems that are dynamic within and between subsystems and that are constantly changing at the level of the whole.

FIGURE 6.4
Mechanistic and Organic Systems

Mechanistic Systems	Organic Systems
• *static*: change is detrimental, new improved models replace old	• *dynamic*: growth and change are normal, development over time
• *linear causality*: change begins at one point and affects other areas	• *multidirectional causality*: change begins at different places and produces feedback loops
• *grow old*: wear down and break down	• *reproduce*: produce new living things

flying beings. In flight they constantly move their wings, feathers, and body shape to adjust their flight. So birds' ability to change is their strength.

Second, internal changes in organisms affect the whole system. They can be initiated in any of the parts or subsystems, and they affect all the other systems as well as the system of systems as a whole. In fact, there is a positive feedback loop that is the defining property of nonlinear systems. Living systems do not simply operate, they change, grow, and develop. In this respect, the parts of the system are active in shaping the whole. In the study of social systems, this fact introduces moral issues because the "parts" are living beings, not inanimate objects.

Third, change in living systems is due to their changing relationships with their environments. Brody and Sobel remark, "Living systems are continuously exchanging matter, energy, and information with their environments and must periodically adapt their inner activities to accommodate changes in the environment. Environment is simply and relatively defined as everything outside the boundaries of the system" (1979, 7). This ability to change in response to the environment is what we mean by adaptation.

Finally, new components introduced into a system are normally reinterpreted within the framework of the system in order to save energy. The system itself is reluctant to change structurally to accommodate the new components. So, for example, when pills were first introduced to Papua New Guinea tribals, they saw these as new and more powerful forms of magic. This saved them from the enormous effort that would have been involved in restructuring their views on disease and medicine.

Levels of Systems

In looking at living systems, we find different levels of organization. Human organs are made up of different cells, each of which is born, lives, serves its function in the whole system, and dies. Organs, in turn, can be viewed as subsystems within the human biophysical body. Similarly the physical, biological, psychological, and spiritual parts of a human interact to form a whole person. But people are not autonomous beings. They are products of, and contribute to, corporate human systems: social systems that organize them into societies and cultural systems that encode their beliefs, feelings, and values. To this we need to add spiritual systems, for humans are spiritual beings and, therefore, relate to angels and fallen angels and to God, the source of all creation.

Ultimately, in exegeting humans it is important that we take a system-of-systems approach rather than reductionist or stratigraphic approach (fig. 6.5). We must recognize that change can be initiated in any of the systems or subsystems and that such changes affect all other human systems. Moreover, when changes take place we must differentiate between cause and effect. For example, biological problems such as illness can cause disruption in our family (social system) and eventually force us to reexamine our theological explanations (cultural system) and our prayer life (spiritual system). Similarly, living in known sin can cause biological, social, and cultural symptoms. In examining humans individually and corporately, it may be difficult to find the root cause for the changes; it is easier to treat symptoms with the hope that the problem will go away. But we must identify causes accurately if we are to be effective in our ministries.

FIGURE 6.5
A Systems Approach to the Study of Humans

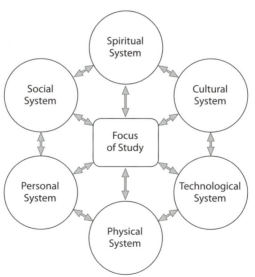

Human systems are influenced by changes in the external environment. On the one hand, climate changes can radically alter the social, cultural, and personal lives of a society. On the other hand, changes in human systems affect the external environment, for instance, through deforestation and urban spread. Taking a system-of-systems approach reminds us of our interconnectedness with the whole of God's creation.

A system-of-systems approach is difficult to maintain. There is always the tendency to make one or another system or subsystem foundational to the others. Economists treat economics as foundational. Sociologists treat social structure and social process as foundational. Christians are in danger of treating the spiritual life as the only important one. A true system-of-systems approach must identify levels of subsystems from the ground up—biological, psychological, social, cultural, and spiritual—but it must do so recognizing the importance of all of them.

In our analysis of human contexts, we will focus on social and cultural systems, although these must be seen in relationship to physical, psychological, and spiritual systems as well. We will focus on synchronic approaches to exegeting humans, but we must keep in mind that humans live in contexts that are constantly being shaped by history. These histories are particular and need to be studied in every case to complement our structural understanding (fig. 6.6).

FIGURE 6.6
A Systems Approach in Historical Context

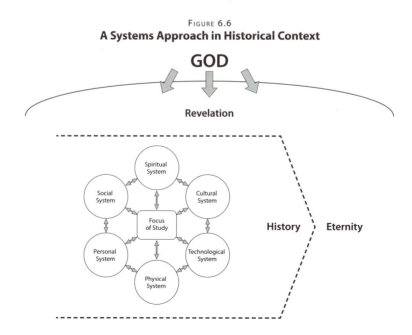

Social Systems

All humans live in societies, or communities of humans, who relate to one another in orderly ways. Without some social order, human life is impossible. Even the ascetics living alone in the desert were given life and nurtured by other humans.

Each community creates its own order. That order is the result of human interactions that, over time, lead to socially acceptable ways of doing things. Patterns emerge as people relate, imitate one another, learn from their parents, or are forced to behave in certain ways by those who hold power over them. Patterns help people understand what is going on and know how to behave in different situations. Social order makes community life both possible and meaningful.

Social systems are not static. They are contested by different parts of the community, males and females, rich and poor, high caste and low caste. They are reinforced or changed every time humans interact. When, as church members, we let Pastor John preach on Sunday morning, we are acknowledging that he is our pastor and we are his parishioners. If we someday decide he is no longer our pastor, we will prevent him from leading church services. We may even decide we want a lay pastor and so change the social order of the church.

Order varies greatly from one society to another. In small bands it is based largely on ties of kinship and personal acquaintance. In modern cities social organization has many layers and is based more on institutions, voluntary associations, and networks. Relationships are less personal and are based on contract and law, not intimate personal knowledge of one another.

Social Structures

Human social systems are complex. We need only look at a modern city to see this. How do fifteen million people and more live together to form an urban society such as Mexico City, Beijing, or Calcutta? To understand how these societies function as social systems, we need to examine first their structure, then their functions.

LEVELS OF SOCIAL ORGANIZATION

Societies are organized into several different levels. At the lowest level, all human societies are based on countless transactions among individuals. At the intermediate level, people form groups to accomplish certain tasks.

At the highest level, complex social systems emerge that enable people and groups to live together in large societies and the world. Here, we examine the levels of social organization from the ground up in more detail.

STATUS AND ROLE

The basis of society is the interaction among individuals in everyday life. A mother scolds her child, two friends play golf, and a shopper writes a check for merchandise. In each of these relationships much is unique to the individuals and situation. Each mother, child, friend, shopper, and clerk is unique, and each transaction has its own historical context. But the behavior in each of these settings must also fit socially defined patterns understood by all parties if the relationship is to continue. If the mother scolds her child in a socially unacceptable way, others will intervene. If the shopper walks out of the store without paying for the goods, the community, through its police, will enforce its rules with socially defined sanctions.

A pair of concepts helps us to understand these basic social transactions: *status* and *role*. Status is a socially defined position in a society. In American society, for example, statuses include mother, son, doctor, plumber, teacher, pastor, pilot, and so on. In South India they include *brahmin* (high-caste Hindu), *vaidudu* (a type of doctor), and *mantrakar* (magician). Each society has its own sets of statuses. It is important to separate in our minds social structures from real people. Real people occupy statuses, but the statuses exist apart from these people. For example, a church may have a status called pastor. There may be no one in that status at the moment, but it remains as a position in the church while the church is looking for someone to fill it.

Real people must occupy one or more statuses in society to be a part of it. A person may be a child, lawyer, teacher, or any other status recognized by the group. But he or she cannot function without a status. If a stranger appears, we do not know who she is or how to relate to her until we can place her in one of the statuses we recognize. One of these statuses may be foreigner or invader. In any case, we will know how to respond only when we know which status is being occupied.

Each status is associated with a set of roles—the patterns of behavior that we expect of those who occupy that status in relation to others. The pastor must preach, the shopper must pay the clerk, and the driver must drive on the right side of a two-way highway. If people do not behave properly, they are disciplined or removed from their statuses.

Statuses in a society are linked to each other to form paired relationships. For example, the position of teacher is linked to that of student, husband to wife, and employer to employee. Most statuses, in fact, are linked to more than one other status in paired roles. As teachers, we relate to students, principals, parents, other teachers, and the public. The teacher acts differently toward a student than he or she does toward the principal and in yet another way toward the parents of the students.

To illustrate the usefulness of status and role in examining social organizations, let us look at the American nuclear family. It is made up of eight statuses (husband, wife, mother, father, daughter, son, sister, brother) and eight possible pairs of relationships (fig. 6.7). A family with only one child does not have a full set of family relationships. By contrast, a large family may have several instances of any particular relationship.

FIGURE 6.7
Statuses and Roles in a Nuclear Family

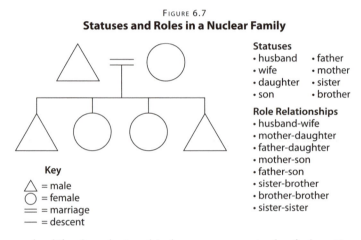

Statuses
- husband   • father
- wife   • mother
- daughter   • sister
- son   • brother

Role Relationships
- husband-wife
- mother-daughter
- father-daughter
- mother-son
- father-son
- sister-brother
- brother-brother
- sister-sister

Key
△ = male
○ = female
= = marriage
— = descent

In everyday life, the relationship between a particular father, Tom Smith, and his sons, John and Henry, will vary according to their individual personalities and the specific settings in which they interact. From a social point of view, however, we look for the common range of patterns underlying all father-son relationships in a given society. For example, many North Americans believe a husband should treat older and younger sons alike. The oldest should not be favored or get all of the inheritance. In other societies, fathers are expected to favor their oldest sons, as was true of the Old Testament Israelites. In those societies, treating them all as equal would be illegitimate.

Using status and role analysis, we can examine the social organization of a family system. We can also trace historical changes in that system. For example, the relationship between husband and wife is currently being redefined in our society. This affects the other relationships in the family, such as mother-child and father-child.

It is important to remember that each society has its own set of statuses and roles. Even such basic relationships as husband-wife, father-son, and mother-daughter are different in different societies. For instance, a Trobriand Island father gives the yams he raises to his sister to support her and her children. He, his wife, and his children live on the yams brought to him by his wife's brothers. To him, this arrangement seems as natural as parents working to earn money to support their own nuclear family seems to us.

NETWORKS

Interpersonal relationships are the basis of all social activity. Linked together, they give rise to the simplest form of social organization, namely, the network. A social network is a web of relationships that links people to one another. For example, John knows Mary, George, and Tina (fig. 6.8). Mary knows Julius and Margaret. Margaret knows Sarah. A network is not a social group because those in the network do not all know and interact with one another. Sarah, for instance, knows only Margaret and George, but not John, Julius, Mary, or Tina.

FIGURE 6.8
Social Networks

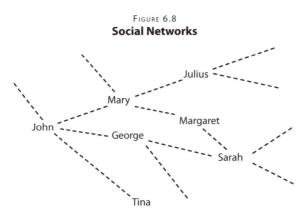

Social networks are important as channels of communication. In all societies people get important information through gossip and word of mouth. Moreover, networks are an important means of social control. John may not like what Julius is doing and may say this to Mary, knowing that Mary is Julius's friend. This second-hand communication allows messages to be sent without the volatility latent in direct confrontation.

Networks do play an important part in the formation of social groups. If John organizes a party, he invites George, Mary, and Tina. Mary asks if she can bring her friend Julius. At the party, these people all get to know one another and plan to meet weekly for lunch. Sarah is part of the larger network, but she is not a part of the group because she does not interact directly with the others.

GROUPS

At the next level up we can analyze social organization in terms of the kinds of groups that people form. A group is a set of people who relate to one another face to face for specific purposes. For example, people in a local church form a group because they belong to the same congregation. In their church they have smaller groups such as classes, committees, and cliques. Groups enable people to join together to accomplish common goals. People may gather together to organize a factory, a school, or a recreational club. In each of these, they must create statuses and roles and link these together to form a single social system.

Groups fall into three basic types depending on the nature of the relationships on which they are built: kinship, geography, and association. Kinship groups are based on ties of marriage and descent. The primary kinship group is the nuclear family, made up of husbands, wives, and their children. In many societies families include either several wives (polygyny), or several husbands (polyandry), so the nuclear family is larger than it is in the West.

Extended families are made up of several nuclear families linked together by blood and marriage. In India, for example, extended families include aged parents, their married sons and grandsons and their families, and their unmarried daughters and granddaughters. These all live and work together and often share a common kitchen and household. With few notable exceptions, families are the basic building blocks of all societies.[2]

On a larger scale, kinship ties are used to organize lineages and clans. A lineage is a group of people known to be linked to one another by blood ties through either male or female descent. A patrilineage is made up of men linked through male descent to a common known forefather. Usually their wives and unmarried daughters are also members of their lineage. A matrilineage is made up of women traceable through female lines to a common ancestress, plus their husbands and children.

Patriclans and matriclans are the same, except that the lines of descent fade into myth as one goes back to the founding ancestors. In other words,

---

2. One exception is the Nayar society of Kerala, in South India. In the past, Nayar women had sexual relationships with Brahmin men from the highest caste, but could not marry them. The women formed households with their brothers, who helped them rear their children.

these are groups of people who believe they are linked to one another through common blood ties to some distant progenitor, but who cannot actually trace the links. Often there is a myth of common origin, and the founder of the clan may be thought to have been a god or an animal. Lineages and clans are powerful ways to organize large groups to carry out community tasks such as crop production, defense, government, and social welfare.

The highest level of kinship organization is a tribe or an ethnic community. The former exists more or less by itself, the latter with other ethnic communities in a larger society. Both tribes and ethnic communities include people who believe they are the same kind of people because they share the same kind of blood and marry one another. Marriage to someone of another blood is perceived as threatening to the ethnic group. Because tribes and other ethnic communities can be large, numbering even in the millions, we will examine them under societal categories.

People believe ethnicity is based on genetic ties, but it is important to remember that these beliefs do not always match biological realities. In any case, what matters is the social interpretation of biological ties. A great many social mechanisms, such as adoption, surrogate marriages, and fictive descent, override genetics. Ultimately, all societies choose to define some genetic ties as kin and to deny or ignore other such ties.

A second kind of group is based on geographic proximity—people who relate to one another because they live in a common place. The smallest stable geographic group is the community. The members of a community live out their daily lives and deal with the common problems of everyday life together. Examples of this are a nomadic camp, a village, and a neighborhood in a city. Larger geographic groups are cities, nation-states, regional alliances, and, increasingly, the earth "webbed together" as one world.

A third kind of group is made up of people who gather or organize on the basis of a common interest (such as clubs), common tasks (such as schools and work crews), or common identity (ethnic and alumni associations). Groups may be organized on more than one of these principles. For instance, the German Baptist Church uses both ethnicity and association as the basis for its organization. The German Baptist Church of Mount City also uses geography to define its identity.

Some groups, such as crowds, audiences, and mobs, are temporary gatherings that are loosely organized. Others, such as clubs, professional associations, and churches, are more formally organized and endure over time. Membership may be voluntary, as in a sandlot baseball team, or coerced, as in a drafted army. Admission may be open to all or restricted to a few.

Associations are extremely flexible. They are readily organized for any common purpose, and members can be added or dropped quite easily. This makes it possible for people to move from one place to another and to change their social ties rapidly. Moreover, a simple gathering can be organized into an enduring association that may grow into a complex institution, such as a business corporation or political party. Because of their flexibility, associations have emerged as the dominant form of social group in modern, complex societies.

As societies grow larger, associations develop into institutions, and complex social systems emerge that enable people to organize increasingly complex economic and political systems. An association, such as a local flying club, can grow into a major airline with a vast array of personnel, ground workers, planes, and technical services. Similarly, a local factory may grow into a multinational business conglomerate. In the process of this growth, what starts as a social group ends up as a complex organization that links many groups of people together. An airline, for instance, develops relationships with other institutions that manufacture planes, supply fuel, maintain airports, sell tickets, provide insurance coverage, produce meals, and deliver late luggage, to name a few.

Large institutions, such as banks, industrial corporations, governments, armies, universities, denominations, and medical systems, are the backbone of modern social organization above the level of families, communities, and associations. Institutions develop their own internal social organizations and subcultures and provide people in urban settings with much of their social identity.

Societal Categories

Societal categories are parts of the mental maps people have of their society. For example, in the United States we mentally group citizens as Democrats, Republicans, and independents. And we categorize them as Christians, Jews, Muslims, Hindus, and so on. These categories help us think about the way society is ordered.

Societal categories shape social relationships. In North America, being middle class rather than lower class, or Democrat rather than Republican, affects how we behave. It also influences the way we are treated and the way we treat others. Societal categories give rise to social groups. People who are Republicans organize local caucuses (social groups) and try to influence the Republican Party (the national institution).

There are three types of societal categories that should be noted here: *ethnicity*, *class*, and *gender*. As we have seen, an ethnic group consists of people who share a consciousness that they are the same kind of people because they share the same blood. In other words, they believe they have common ancestors, share a history, and are linked by ties of descent and marriage. Ethnicity as a societal category divides a society into different types of people. People of the same ethnicity turn to one another for mutual support and base their identity on the larger category of which they are a part. They usually look at people in other ethnic communities as outsiders.

Classes are sets of people who have in common a certain sort of occupation, range of income, and lifestyle. In North America, people of the same class live in similar homes, drive similar cars, go to similar clubs, have similar interests, and share similar values. They feel comfortable with others in their class. They are in what Robert Bellah (1985, 335) calls "life-style enclaves."[3] While identity in ethnic groups is largely ascribed, identity in classes is based partly on achievement. Consequently, there is more social mobility in classes. People who work hard can rise to higher classes, and those who fail can drop to a lower class.

Gender differences are fundamental to all social systems. The normative relationship between men and women varies from culture to culture, but all societies categorize people as one or the other for social purposes.

Societies

The largest unit in social organization is the whole society. Societies are composed of the people who belong to one social system and one territory. The boundaries of a society are often fuzzy, and it is sometimes easier to define its core than to delimit its edges. One way to determine where the boundaries are is to take note of how people greet one another. People from other societies are greeted as strangers and outsiders, rather than as insiders. Armies from the outside are fought as enemies. Thus while killing is considered to be murder if it takes place among insiders, it is praised and rewarded if it occurs outside.

In small societies, a single ethnic group constitutes a whole society, and everyone speaks the same language, shares the same culture, and occupies the same territory. We refer to these societies as bands and tribes.[4] Bands

---

3. Bellah defines these as follows: "A lifestyle enclave is formed by people who share some feature of private life. Members of a lifestyle enclave express their identity through shared patterns of appearance, consumption, and leisure activities, which often serve to differentiate them sharply from those with other lifestyles" (1985, 335).

4. Unfortunately, in some parts of the world the word *tribe* is considered demeaning and associated with notions such as primitive, backward, and uncivilized. In other parts of the

are organized at the level of the nuclear family, and tribes are organized by lineages. But in both cases the society as a whole shares a common ethnicity.

Peasant societies are larger and are made up of multiple ethnic groups and classes. For example, Indian villages organize castes (which have many of the characteristics of ethnic groups) and classes into relatively autonomous, yet structurally complex, agricultural communities. Such villages have clear geographic and social boundaries. They are, in this sense, whole societies. Still, there are people living at the edges of a village society. Gypsies and tribals may live in separate hamlets and be marginal members of the village. Traders, government officials, religious leaders, pilgrims, and many others constantly pass through the village, but do not belong there. They are representatives of the larger external society.

Cities, by contrast, have less clear social boundaries. They are made up of many ethnic groups and lifestyle enclaves networked together. They may be politically and territorially defined, but they transcend these boundaries as they grow. Urban centers, in particular, shape and are shaped by their sociocultural contexts and by the larger society.

Increasingly, the world itself is being networked into a global society. There are, in fact, many globalizations that ally and compete for global power and prestige: economic, political, academic, and religious (Berger and Huntington 2003). Today, few societies on earth are unaffected by this emergence of global systems.

Dimensions of Social Systems

All human relationships and social organizations have four primary dimensions: social, economic, political, and legal. One or another of these may be the focus in a given relationship or organization, but the others are always present in the background (fig. 6.9). For example, people gather in church for social fellowship and for worship, but the church must also have economic, political, and legal structures in order to function.

SOCIAL

By social we mean the definition, nature, allocation, and use of relationships. This includes the statuses and roles of those involved. It also includes

---

world, such as India, ethnic groups are proud to be known as tribes because it distances them from the caste system. Because in anthropology the word *tribe* is a technical term with positive connotations, I use it here.

FIGURE 6.9
Dimensions of Social Relationships

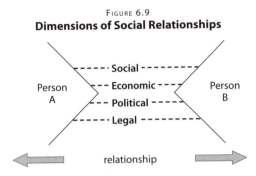

the types of social and societal groups people form, their institutions, and their larger societal systems.

Some relationships are egalitarian; others are hierarchical. Some are informal; others are formal (that is, they are carefully regulated by rules of etiquette and order). Some are temporary and others are lasting. All these factors are part of the social dimension of relationships and structures.

ECONOMIC

Economics has to do with the definition, nature, allocation, and use of resources. All societies use material resources. As part of daily life, people plow fields, catch fish, build houses, ride horses, and make music. They heat their houses, fly in planes, and communicate by electromagnetic waves. To do so they create tools that enable them to shape the world around them. These natural assets, tools, and products are among the people's economic resources. Economic resources also include intangible assets such as the people's labor, time, specialized knowledge, the right to sing a song, and magical powers. Each society defines for itself what it sees as economic resources.

Each society also decides who owns the resources and who can use them. For instance, in our society fish in most lake areas are a common resource, which means the fish that are caught are owned by the people who catch them. In many migrant band societies, no one owns the land or trees, so anyone can use them, though they must do so responsibly. In agricultural villages, land is one of the most valued commodities and usually can be owned out right. Among the Eskimos, only the writer of a song is free to sing it. Others must ask permission to do so. Notions of the ownership of resources vary widely and are part of the economic dimension of relationships and structures.

POLITICAL

Politics involves the definition, nature, allocation, and use of power. Power is an essential part of all human relationships. It is the ability to persuade or influence through prestige or moral authority. On the one hand, it is physical coercion and the ability to destroy another, or the ability to care for the vulnerable. On the other hand, it includes the power of the weak to ignore, disobey, boycott, and badger.

In ordinary relationships, power is hidden because everyone plays by the social rules. If the social order itself is challenged, however, power is often exercised to reestablish it. For example, people may demonstrate in the streets against a government, which then uses its police and army to crush the rebellion. The allocation and use of power is the political dimension of relationships and structures.

LEGAL

The fourth dimension of human relationships and social systems is law. This has to do with the definition, nature, allocation, and use of legitimacy. Legitimacy is the people's consent to let certain persons have and use power.[5] A person may use power to take control of a situation, but if that person does not have the publicly recognized authority to do so, the act is viewed as a revolution. If the person acts as a recognized leader, the actions will be considered part and parcel of normal government.

The allocation of legitimacy varies greatly from society to society. In ancient Egypt it was thought to be given by the gods and allocated to the Pharaoh by birth. In dictatorships it is based on conquest followed by rituals of legitimization. In democratic societies it is given to the rulers directly by the vote of the people.

The nature of legitimacy, too, varies greatly. In some monarchies the ruler has absolute power. In many democracies the leader is subject to a constitution and a body of law. In stateless societies there are no formal governing bodies. In these societies, governmental functions are allocated to other social institutions such as clans, villages, and age-based associations. Thus the nature and allocation of legitimacy is the legal dimension of relationships and structures.

---

5. People do not have to like the leaders or agree with what they are doing to consider them legitimate. As long as people believe that these leaders should be in power, or at least are not willing to make the effort to depose them, the leaders will have enough legitimacy to rule. Not all Americans like the president of the United States or his policies, but most of them do consider him the legitimate leader of the country.

Politics and law are closely related to one another. Power without legitimacy is coercive. It is revolution. Power with legitimacy is government. So when revolutions succeed, they seek to add legitimacy to their rule. A careful analysis of human relationships shows that normally both power and legitimacy are needed and present.

It would be a mistake to assume that the four dimensions act independently from one another. All are present in every human relationship and social organization, and each affects the others. At times it is hard to differentiate between them. For instance, high social status may enable a person to gain wealth or political power. Conversely, political leaders may be able to convert their power into social prestige and wealth.

A simple example of the interaction between the dimensions of social systems can be seen in the relationship between a mother and her daughter. Socially, their statuses are "mother" and "daughter." They are, therefore, expected to act in certain ways toward each other. These patterns of behavior are their roles. Because of her status, however, the mother controls many resources the child wants: the mother's attention, candy in the jar, and permission to stay up late. Politically, the mother can pressure her daughter to obey by giving commands, offering rewards, or, if necessary, by using force. Legally the society recognizes the mother's right to use this power and will not intervene except when the mother goes beyond the socially recognized use of force. In the evening the child wants to watch television, but the mother wants to read her a Bible story. The disagreement is over which task to do. The child exercises her power by crying. The mother negotiates a compromise, such as allowing some of each.

Power, authority, resources, tasks, and interpersonal contact are all intertwined in this social relationship. Still, at any given moment one or another of the dimensions may be the focus of the relationship. When the mother and daughter read the Bible together they are engaged in cultural communication. When the daughter refuses and cries, she initiates a power confrontation, and the Bible study cannot continue until the issue of power to make decisions is resolved.

This type of analysis can also be applied to human groups. People organize a church to worship God and to communicate the gospel to the world. But these religious purposes are accomplished through relationships that include the four dimensions. The church has a social aspect. Members seek statuses in the congregation and gather in fellowship. The church must deal with the economic dimension of life: buildings, salaries, volunteer time, and copyrights on songs. It must also deal with political issues such as leadership selection and the use of power. Legally it is internally regulated by its constitution, bylaws, and rules of order; it is externally regulated by government zoning laws, noise regulations, and lawsuits. It is impossible to organize a church that focuses only on worship and witness and is free from economic, political, social, and legal concerns.

Human activities focus on specific purposes, tasks, and goals at hand. People work together to build a road, run a shop, choose a leader, or worship God. In the process they relate to one another using resources, power, and legitimacy. In a marriage, the social function is in the forefront. In other activities, other dimensions are central. But all relationships have aspects of the four dimensions.

Institutions, too, are organized for specific functions. Political groups focus their attention directly on the control of power, but in the process they must deal with economic, legal, and social matters. Banks, factories, and businesses are concerned primarily with economic matters. Government bodies deal mainly with legal matters. But businesses and governments also have a social dimension. All four dimensions are present in all institutions.

Cultural Systems

The second system we examine is culture. There are many anthropological definitions of culture. Here we will define it as the more or less integrated system of beliefs, feelings, and values created and shared by a group of people that enable them to live together socially and that are communicated by means of their systems of symbols and rituals, patterns of behavior, and the material products they make.

Constructed and Contested

Culture is shared by a community of people. It is constructed by people in the course of living together. Humans are social creatures and depend on one another for survival and a meaningful existence. They need care during their childhood and in their old age. They find their greatest joy and fulfillment in the company of others. Social isolation is among the greatest punishments they inflict on one another. Thus, all human relationships require a large measure of shared understanding between people. They need a common language and some consensus on beliefs and worldview for communication and coordinated action. Ultimately, their culture is the home in which they live together.

Cultures are more or less integrated systems. This means that they provide us with a more or less coherent way of looking at things. If our belief systems contradict one another too much, we are torn by cognitive dissonance and the fear of meaninglessness. Integration, however, is never complete. In part, this is because cultures constantly change. New ideas are introduced that run counter to old ideas, and tensions emerge. For instance, the development of the computer and the World Wide Web has radically changed the way we communicate with one another around the world. The art of handwriting long, beautifully composed letters is dying. This is probably changing the way we communicate and even the notion of relationship itself.

Ultimately, cultures are constructed by societies and may be contested within them. Groups and individuals in a culture can hold different beliefs. The rich, for example, see things differently from the poor, and one ethnic group may view the world differently from another. There are differences between the folk beliefs of the common people and the theories of specialists in the fields of religion and medicine. Different communities in the same society struggle to control the society. For example, in the United States there are bodies of people for and against abortion, homosexuality, going to war, and giving the government more or less power.

If a culture loses its ability to provide a framework for the existence of a corporate way of life that makes sense to the people and thus no longer meets their basic need for coordinated activity, then the culture disintegrates. We see this when societies are overrun by other, more powerful ones or collapse internally.

Dimensions of Culture

Cultures express human beliefs, feelings, and morals (fig. 6.10). The cognitive dimension includes the beliefs and knowledge shared by the members of a group or society. Without shared beliefs, communication and community life are impossible. Beliefs link categories into theories of explanation. For instance, Americans speak of malaria, smallpox, diphtheria, and cancer and believe these are produced by natural causes. In South India, villagers attribute the *hot* and *cold* diseases they experience to the anger of female spirits, such as Maisamma and Poshamma, who have not received the sacrifices they expect. The Tiv of Nigeria attribute many of their illnesses to angry ancestors. Our cultural knowledge tells us how to repair and drive cars, how to bake cakes, how to rear children, how to make an atomic bomb, and how to worship God. A Bushman's knowledge enables him to find giraffe and to kill them with poisonous arrows.

Cultural information is stored in different ways. Many cultures store it in writing. We turn to books, newspapers, billboards, and the Internet to retrieve it. Other cultures store most of their information in stories, songs, riddles, and other forms of oral tradition that are easily remembered.

The affective dimension of culture has to do with the people's emotions, notions of beauty, tastes in food and dress, likes and dislikes, and ways of expressing joy and sorrow. People in one culture like their food spicy, in another they like it sweet or bland. Members of some societies like to express their emotions and are aggressive; in other societies they learn to be self-controlled and calm. Some religions encourage the use of meditation, mysticism, and drugs to achieve inner peace and tranquility. Others stress ecstasy through dance, drums, and self-torture. Still others evoke feelings of awe and fear. In short, cultures vary greatly in how they deal with the emotional side of human life. People are rarely content with a purely utilitarian approach to life. They decorate their pots and baskets, embroider their cloth, paint their houses and bodies, carve their tools, and hang jewelry of all sorts on their bodies. Their houses follow architectural tastes; their evenings are spent in song and dance; their lore is full of stories, poetry, proverbs, and riddles. All reflect the human penchant for self-expression and aesthetic enjoyment. It is difficult to imagine what a society would be like without this expressive culture that pervades all areas of life—without art, music and dance, or sports and games; with undyed clothes, unpainted houses, and only work to break the boredom.

The evaluative or normative dimension of culture has to do with judgments of proper and improper behavior for men, for women, and for children. It includes the moral code that determines what is legal and illegal,

FIGURE 6.10
Dimensions of Culture

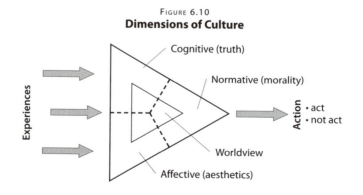

righteous and sinful. For example, in North America it is worse to tell a lie than to hurt a person's feelings. In other cultures, however, it is more important to encourage a person, even if this means bending the truth.

These three dimensions of human experience—ideas, feelings, and values—are important in understanding the nature of humans, their societies, and their cultures. All three are present in every human relationship, though one may be dominant and the others suppressed until some event triggers their release. In planting churches we need to keep all three in mind, for the gospel has to do with all of them. The cognitive level has to do with knowledge and truth—with understanding and trust in biblical and theological information and knowledge of God. The affective dimension includes feelings of worship, love, joy, and peace. The moral dimension has to do with holiness and sin, allegiance to Christ or to self or to other idols.

All three cultural dimensions are essential in conversion. We need to know that Jesus is the Son of God who died for our sins. But that knowledge alone is not enough, for even Satan knows that Jesus is God incarnate. We need feelings of affection for and loyalty to Jesus. But knowledge and feelings must lead us to decide to turn and to follow Christ as the Lord of our lives. Then he will save us.

All three dimensions are also important in building the church. In our services we need sound doctrines, deep feelings, and repentance of sin. We do not proclaim the gospel simply to inform people or to make them feel good. We call them to become lifelong followers of Jesus Christ. So beliefs, feelings, and morals are all important in Christian ministry.

LEVELS OF CULTURE

Cultures have many levels (fig. 6.11). We can see the various products people make and use in their societies, their behavior with and toward one another (i.e., manners, etiquette), their methods of communicating, and their styles of performance in informal and formal rituals. Unseen are sets of beliefs about all the essential domains of life: beliefs about raising crops, building houses, diseases and medicines, the family and ancestors, and gods and supernatural powers. Moreover, underlying these are implicit worldviews.

MATERIAL CULTURE

Culture is most visible in the products people make. These include baskets, houses, bows and arrows, musical instruments, cars, and other material goods. They also include modifications of the environment such

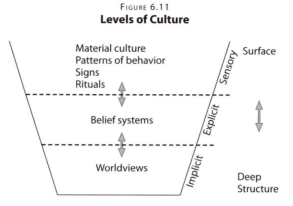

Figure 6.11
Levels of Culture

as digging ditches and plowing fields. The variety of human material creations is almost impossible to catalog. These cultural products show us the knowledge people have of the material world, and often manifest deep assumptions about the nature of that reality. The way people orient and design rooms in their houses and the layouts they use in constructing roads give us deep insight into how they view space.

Patterns of Behavior

Another way culture is visible is in the patterns of behavior (manners, behavioral norms, etiquette) shared by the people of a society: how they greet one another, the way they drive, the way they cook their food, the way they divide labor, and the way they relate to one another and to strangers. It is not incidental behavior that concerns us here but the behavioral patterns that are prescribed by the society.

Signs and Sign System

Our knowledge of the world around us is rooted in an unending flow of experiences, each of which is unique. To make sense of these (given the limits of the human brain), we need to reduce them to a limited number of categories, so we create words that lump a great many experiences into one. We see many different objects and label them all "trees." We see a great many people, each of whose face is distinct, and call them "humans." It is this ability to generalize and to create languages that enables us to think about the world and decide on courses of action.

Humans are unique among earthly creatures in this ability to create a universe of symbols and to live in this universe that we create in our minds: "Except in the immediate satisfaction of biological needs, man lives in a world not of things but of symbols" (von Bertalanffy 1981, 1). We create images or maps of the external world that we use to think about the world and then to act in it. We manipulate these maps to think of other possibilities and to work to achieve these visions. We imagine a house, draw up blueprints, and then build it. We think of distant friends and phone them. In short, we use our mental images to understand the past, to live in the present, and to plan for the future.

This ability to construct mental maps of the external world is based on our ability to create signs. A sign is anything that stands for something else in the mind of a person or a group of people (fig. 6.12). We see real trees and construct a generalized mental image of them. Then we create the spoken word *tree* to represent that image. Thereafter, when we hear the word *tree* we retrieve the mental image of the real trees we have seen. We use facial expressions to communicate feelings, lines to create lanes on roads, bells to announce worship, and perfumes and flowers to speak of love.

FIGURE 6.12
Nature of Signs

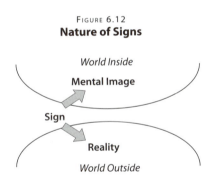

Signs are building blocks that enable humans to construct mental worlds of reality. We use these inner worlds to live in the external world and to manipulate it. In our minds we think of our house and drive to it. We can also think of things we have not experienced. We mentally picture a purple cow, so we paint a toy cow purple. We imagine flying and build airplanes to do so. Symbols enable us to manipulate the world internally and then to reshape the world externally. In short, it is this ability to create signs that enables us as humans to think, to live, and to communicate with one another about the world in which we live. Mary Douglas describes the process:

> As perceivers we select from all the stimuli falling on our senses only those
> which interest us, and our interests are governed by a pattern-making ten-

dency. . . . In a chaos of shifting impressions, each of us constructs a stable world in which objects have recognizable shapes, are located in depth, and have permanence. In perceiving we are building, taking some cues and rejecting others. The most acceptable cues are those which fit most easily into the pattern that is being built up. . . . As time goes on and experiences pile up, we make a greater and greater investment in our systems of labels. So a conservative bias is built in. It gives us confidence. At any time we may have to modify our structure of assumptions to accommodate new experience, but the more consistent experience is with the past, the more confidence we can have in our assumptions . . . by and large anything we take note of is pre-selected and organized in the very act of perceiving. (1966, 36–37)

Signs are not isolated units. They are parts of larger sets and systems. In English we speak of the color red. This belongs to our taxonomy of colors: red, orange, yellow, green, blue, and violet. So when we say an object is "red," we are also saying that it is not orange, yellow, green, blue, or violet. Different cultures create different taxonomies and, as we will see later, these taxonomies reflect and reinforce the underlying worldviews. To understand worldviews as parts of cultural systems, it is important to study the visible signs people use to reflect their beliefs, feelings, and values.

RITUALS

People express their deepest beliefs, feelings, and values in rituals. Rituals range from simple rites such as shaking hands, blowing a kiss, or embracing to banquets, fiestas, weddings, funerals, New Year's celebrations, memorials, parades for heads of state, and sacred ceremonies held in churches, temples, and mosques. Modern people tend to view these rituals as harmless interludes or discount them as meaningless performances. But rituals play a central role in most societies, revealing to us the basic assumptions underlying their cultures. They are multilayered transactions in which speech and behavior are socially prescribed.

On one level, rituals give visible expression to the social norms that order relationships between people as they form families, groups, communities, and societies. On another level, they give visible expression to the deep cultural norms that order the way people think, feel, and evaluate their worlds. They communicate what words alone cannot, such as deep feelings and mysteries. They give public expression to the moral order that people believe was created by the gods, defined by ancestors, or instituted by the culture's heroes when they taught people to be civilized and human. Rituals make explicit human experiences in the form of stories by reenacting them. They are dramas enacted in arenas that are set apart from everyday life and call to attention the deeper structures and meanings of life itself.

Rituals can be divided into three major types: rites of intensification, rites of passage, and rites of crisis. The first type celebrates the common life of the group and renews the deep beliefs of the participants in their culture. Rites of intensification include harvest festivals, New Year's celebrations, and the like. The second type celebrates the movement of individuals from one stage of life to another. Rites of passage include birth, adulthood, marriage, and death rituals. The third type includes ceremonies that are precipitated by unforseen events, such as plague, drought, war, and other disasters. Rites of crisis include healing rituals, rain dances, and so forth. All types are important means of giving visible expression to the social and cultural beliefs and norms of a society.

Belief Systems

At the heart of a culture are the many belief systems the people share. In contrast to the more visible dimensions we have discussed up to this point, these beliefs may be more implicit, operating beneath the surface. For example, some people attribute illnesses to viruses and bacteria; others to the anger of ancestors; others to curses, broken taboos, and witchcraft; and still others to fate or bad karma. All are logical explanations for reality as perceived by people in a particular context. They are alternative explications for the same set of questions—in this case, "Why do people get sick?"

These low-level theories are imbedded in higher-level systems of knowledge. We will label the higher-level systems "knowledge systems." Knowledge systems are generally made up of at least three key components: (1) a set of key questions and beliefs about the type of entities and processes that make up the domain of inquiry; (2) a set of questions worth asking within the domain; and (3) a set of epistemic and methodological norms about how the domain is to be investigated, how theories are to be tested, and how data are to be collected.

Knowledge systems serve important functions in the generation of theories. They indicate what the people in a particular culture hold as uncontroversial background knowledge; they identify portions of theories that are in difficulty and need modification; they establish rules for the collection of data and the testing of theories; and they challenge theories that violate the foundational assumptions of the tradition (Laudan 1996, 83–84).

An active knowledge system is generally made up of a family of theories, some of which are mutually consistent while other rival theories are not. What these theories have in common is that they seek to answer the same questions and can be tested and evaluated using the methodological norms and data of the research tradition. The sciences, for example—physics, chemistry, biology, medicine, and sociology—are belief systems. In theology, systematic theology and biblical theology are belief systems. Knowledge systems guide thought processes and enable people to focus on experience and formulate theories to help them solve the problems of life and to pursue their goals. In so doing, they help give meaning to life.

Worldviews

People who live in the same society share beliefs, feelings, and values. Underlying these are the categories we create, the logic we use to form a coherent understanding of reality, and the fundamental cognitive, affective, and evaluative assumptions we make about the ultimate nature of things. These largely implicit cognitive substructures constitute our *worldview*. A worldview is the most encompassing view of reality we share with other people in a common culture. It is what we think with, not what we think about. It is the mental picture of reality we use to make sense of the world around us. This worldview is based on deep assumptions about the nature of reality, the "givens" of life. And it clothes itself with an aura of certainty that convinces us that it is, in fact, the true reality. To question a worldview is to challenge the very foundation of life, and we resist such challenges with strong emotional reactions. There are few human fears greater than the fear of a loss of a sense of order and meaning. We are even willing to die for these beliefs because they make death itself meaningful.[6]

Spiritual Systems

Those of us who are influenced by modernity must also begin to see spiritual systems as integral parts of our everyday world. This is particularly hard for us to do, because modernity has relegated the spirit world to the realm of fiction. As Christians, we tend to locate spiritual systems in the heavens, leaving us to live our lives on earth according to the laws of nature. We must take spiritual systems seriously and begin to see how the angels, including the fallen angels, are involved in our everyday human lives. We must remember our own spiritual nature in our calculations and

---

6. For a full analysis of the concept of worldview, see Hiebert 2008.

understandings of human life. Above all else, we must be aware of how God is ever present and acting in all areas of our lives.[7]

A System of Systems

Human physical, biological, psychological, social, cultural, and spiritual systems are interrelated. This is particularly true of social and cultural systems that involve groups of humans living and working together. In general, social systems are patterns and structures of social behavior. Cultural systems interpret that behavior. On the one hand, society shapes culture. We talk to one another and in so doing reinforce and change our language. We organize activities and create rules to do so. We make computers and soon think of the mind as a supercomputer. In everyday life we create and re-create our culture based on changes in society.

On the other hand, culture shapes society. We try to act as good fathers and mothers by doing what our culture tells us "good" fathers and mothers do. We kneel, bow, or hold up our hands in prayer because our culture tells us this is how to worship God. Our cultural knowledge can radically alter the way we live and relate to one another. We re-create our societies based on changes in culture.

Because of this constant interaction between the way we live and the way our culture tells us to live, it is not always easy to distinguish between what is social and what is cultural. Nevertheless, it is helpful for analytical purposes to do so. For instance, every culture prescribes how good fathers and mothers should rear their children, but a particular couple may act differently from the norm. If their social behavior differs too much from the cultural norms, other people in the society will act to stop it. Or they may decide the new way is better and alter the norm to fit new behaviors. Finally, they may appeal to spiritual systems to decide what to do.

A system-of-systems approach in Christian ministries helps us exegete individuals and groups of people. This is an essential step in missional theology—in making the gospel known to humans in their social and cultural contexts.

---

7. For a fuller account of the need for an understanding of spiritual systems, see Hiebert 1982.

7

Research Methods

There is a great lack of systematic, theoretically based research in missions. Science, business, and government invest significant percentages of their budgets in research. Mission leaders and practitioners, with some exceptions,[1] have no programs or budgets for research. Most imitate the practices of others who have gone before, or follow current fads based on anecdotes and untested hypotheses. Where research has been done, it is largely macrodemographic and quantitative (David Barrett and Patrick Johnson) or ethnographic and descriptive (Caleb Project and Joshua Project).[2] The former is helpful primarily for strategists in mission headquarters. But it offers little to the missionary entering a local community. The latter helps missionaries begin to understand their people, but is not grounded in theoretical and theological frameworks that can guide them in how to do their work. It is difficult to persuade mission agencies to spend any significant amount of their funds on systematic research or to use the findings of such research in planning their work. But without good research, we waste many of the resources God has given us—both human and material—to carry out our mission to the world. We must try to make

1. One of the lasting contributions of Donald McGavran was the call for systematic research based on a clearly articulated theory—in his case, church growth. While the theoretical framework underpinning church growth may be questioned, his call for systematic research must be affirmed.

2. One important exception to this is the Korean Research Institute for Mission, directed by Dr. Stephen Moon in Seoul, Korea.

thorough, theoretically based research a central part of our ministry if we want to move beyond the current confusion in missions.

Methods in Missiology

As we have seen, missiology is a discipline that asks the critical question: how should we work to communicate the gospel to people in their historical and sociocultural contexts so that they understand and believe, and so that the gospel becomes a power that transforms individuals and societies to become followers of Christ who manifest his kingdom on earth? To answer this question missiologists must examine what they mean by the gospel. They must draw on systematic theology,[3] which studies the underlying structure (synchronic) of Scripture, and biblical theology,[4] which looks at the underlying story (diachronic) of Scripture. They must also draw on studies of human history and human sociocultural systems. Missiologists must then study how the gospel can be communicated to humans in their many settings.

Thus the study of missiology covers four main areas, each of which has its own central questions, data to be examined, and methods to be used. It examines the place of mission in theology, using the philosophical methods of systematic theology. It looks at the mission of God as a central theme in the unfolding story of God's revelation, using the methods of biblical theology. It studies the history of the missionary outreach of the church throughout history, using the methods of historiography. Finally, it studies human social and cultural systems, using the methods of the human sciences in order to understand how best to communicate the gospel in specific human contexts.[5] In our discussion here we focus on the methods used by the human sciences.

3. Systematic theology helps us understand the biblical worldview but pays little attention to missions, despite the fact that mission is central to the nature of God and his work in creation and salvation. Missions is viewed as "applied" theology, but the methods used for applying theology are not defined. Systematic theology rarely motivates people to go into missions, and it does not answer the theological questions and issues encountered in other cultures, such as dealing with spirit possession and the nature of divine guidance and healing.

4. Unfortunately, neither the study of biblical theology nor church history have been central in motivating people to go out as missionaries. One focuses on Scripture, the other on the history of the church.

5. It is possible that in drawing on the theories and methods of the human sciences, missiology may be in danger of becoming captive to the social sciences. Likewise, systematic theology can become captive to the theories, logic, and methods of Greek philosophy, and biblical theology become captive to the theories, logic, and methods of modern historiography. To think at all

Methods in Exegeting Human Systems

Part of the reason for the lack of missiological research in human studies is that as missiologists we are driven by the needs of the people we serve, and so are committed to activism. We often find it hard to take time to reflect deeply and to develop sound theoretical frameworks for our ministry. Even when research is done, the time spent often conflicts with practice. The danger is that we cut off research too soon and rarely return to it, or we extend research so long that we never get around to ministry. Research and ministry must go hand in hand. Good research opens many doors for ministry, and ministry raises questions that require further research. The two are parallel, ongoing tasks essential to effective outreach.

Research in studying humans has several important uses. First, it helps us gather information for the sake of making informed decisions and to correct the course of our actions. Too often we simply keep doing what we have always done and what others are doing, and we base our decisions on anecdotes rather than on solid information. We need to constantly evaluate our activities and programs in the light of solid research to correct drift and blind routine. Second, good research can help us raise the church's awareness of missions and motivate it to action. Such studies help us see the work better and, thereby, make us aware of the need and possibilities for ministry.

Third, research can help us empower the church we serve to study its own situation and to change. In recent years, we have become increasingly aware that we should do research not only as outside observers but also as insiders helping the church and mission understand itself. Doing research together with people we serve helps build confidence and abilities in them and teaches them how to study and reflect for themselves.

Finally, we need research to see ourselves. Too often we are blind to our own biases and limitations. Self-reflection in research acts like a mirror, for it helps us see our own historical and cultural contexts and how these shape our understanding of missions.

Macro and Micro Research

Broadly speaking, research in the human sciences ranges between the two poles of macro- and microanalysis. The former examines the big picture;

---

we must draw on human theories and their accompanying methods. This is because we, as theologians and missiologists, are humans rooted in history and culture. But we must hold our methods and theories lightly. We dare not absolutize them or make them equal to Scripture, which is divine revelation.

the latter examines specific human situations. Macro research has been called a "balcony" or "helicopter" view of humans. For instance, it studies whole cities or nations. To do so, the researcher must stand "outside" the society to examine its various units (e.g., ethnic groups, classes, migration patterns, and the like) and their relationships to one another. This requires methods to study whole populations, often through sampling. The result is a stress on quantitative methods of analysis. The theoretical perspective and categories are that of the analyst. In this approach we lose sight of individual subjects and their perspectives. We are concerned with broad generalizations.

The other research pole is microanalysis. Micro research seeks to understand the situation from the point of view of the humans involved. This is a "street level" approach to studying people. It requires involvement with humans as individuals (participatory research), and trying to understand the way they view reality (*emic* studies[6]) in contrast to the outside researcher's theories of reality (*etic* studies). This raises profound questions of intercultural hermeneutics and the ability of the researcher to truly understand the world through the eyes of the people he or she studies. It also raises deep questions with respect to the ethics of doing research on humans, because research produces knowledge, and knowledge is power not only in the academy but also in the lives of the people being studied.

Closely related to the macro-micro continuum is the question of the generalizability of the findings. In macro studies, the ideal is to study the whole population. Rarely is this possible, so the study is limited due to the time and resources available for the study. One way to limit a study is to narrow the focus of what is studied to a few variables and to assume that other variables are constant. The variables to be studied are determined by the theory informing the study. The danger here is reductionism—overlooking variables that in fact are significant to the study. The second way to limit a study is to choose a sample from the population that is representative of the whole. Here the methods of sampling become critical, for the validity of the whole study depends on the validity of the sample.

6. The terms *etic* and *emic* were coined by Kenneth Pike of Wycliffe Bible Translators. *Emic* is the way the people we study see reality. Here we study their categories, logic, and explanation systems. *Etic* is the external scientific view of reality based on the careful study and comparison of different cultures. We must avoid assuming that *etic* is true and *emic* is false. First, people believe that their perceptions of reality (*emic*) are true, and to understand them we need to understand their perceptions. Moreover, as Christians we must begin with their *emic* perceptions in order to evangelize and transform their culture. Second, as Christians we need to test the perceptions of science (*etic*) against a biblical understanding of reality. Science, too, has its cultural biases that need to be examined.

Micro studies are ethnographies that examine specific human situations in great detail, with no restriction on the variables that can be introduced to explain the situation. The result is "thick description."[7] This approach avoids the reductionism of macroanalysis, but introduces the problem of too much data to be gathered, analyzed, and interpreted. Also, microanalysis is the study of one case in great depth, which leaves us with little ability to formulate theory, to compare different human cultures, and to formulate generalizations about humankind.

The middle ground between these poles of micro- and macroanalysis examines more than one case or situation. Many anthropologists move beyond single ethnographies to the examination of two or more cases. In this way, anthropologists attempt to formulate broader generalizations about a single culture (e.g., several village studies, to generalize about Indian village life), to compare two or three cultures (e.g., a comparison of Indian and Mexican villages), and to do ethnology—the formulation of broad theories about humans based on the comparison of many cultures. We in missiology also need to do ethnological studies, because such studies help us understand the coming of the missionary and the gospel from outside the culture.

Ethnographic Research

Ethnographic research is essential to our understanding of, and ministry to, all face-to-face communities. Any ministry to them must begin with a deep understanding of their social and cultural systems and their histories. A number of ethnographic methods have been developed to do ethnographies. We examine a few of these here.

Observation

The first method we use when entering a new culture is observation, because it is both possible and natural from the beginning. It is important to make good observations when we first enter a place because the longer we live in a community, the more we tend to overlook the obvious. Intentional, careful, systematic observation should be continued throughout the research.

There are many things we can learn from observation. We can note how people use space. We can draw maps of houses, temples, villages, or regions, noting the various activities associated with different locations. We can map

7. The term was made popular by Clifford Geertz and refers to deep, detailed ethnographies of specific human situations in order to understand the cultures in which they are embedded.

social realities such as different spaces allocated to women and men, upper and lower classes, and different castes. We can map economic realities, such as agricultural lands, housing areas, rivers, and other resources. We can map religious realities such as temples, shrines, festival centers, places where spirits and demons reside, and village ritual boundaries.

We can observe the way people use time: the cycles of agriculture and industry, festivals, and daily activities of women and men. We can look also at sequences—the order in festivals, annual cycles, and stages of life. We can examine cultural artifacts and technology—the things people make and how they make them. We can examine human transactions—the patterns of everyday behavior, rituals, and relationships to outsiders. And we can examine the signs and symbols they use to communicate their ideas—their language, architecture, religious signs, dance, music, art, and decorations.

Systematic observation helps us build relationships and develop trust. When we show interest and respect for people and their way of life and ask them about their creations, we demonstrate appreciation for them. If we come as students with genuine interest, most people are happy to teach us about their ways because they love their way of life and are proud of their culture.

Observations also lead us to preliminary hypotheses we can investigate using other methods. We must not only ask the questions of what, where, and how, but also *why*.

Participant-Observation

As we live with people, we begin to participate in their lives. We buy goods at a shop, have the barber cut our hair, talk to our neighbors, and invite people to our homes. In turn, they begin to invite us to their activities and include us in their lives. This early participation in the lives of people is important, for it is the beginning of relationships that can grow and become strong and intimate. Too often our temptation as outsiders is to withdraw into our own little worlds by reading books and surfing the Internet. Relationships and understandings come only when we leave our own comfort zone to live and interact with a different culture group. We need to hang out at the local restaurant, sit with people in the village square, join in their festivals, and take time at the market to talk to the shopkeeper while making purchases. This is often psychologically and culturally hard for Westerners to do, but it is critical if we are to successfully accomplish our studies and ministries.

At first, we are outsiders who merely observe the public life of the community. But as we participate we begin to see the world through the eyes of the people we are studying and serving. It is vital that we study this inside view. Even if we do not agree with what we observe, it is important that we understand their view of the world because it is that view, not ours, that gives shape to their lives. To study it, we must show deep interest in their beliefs and not judge or criticize their views as foolish. If we are disapproving or make fun of what we learn, people will no longer share with us. Moreover, it is important to remember that our own way of viewing reality is not always right or complete. Understanding their world can help us reevaluate our own.

As we participate in the lives of the people, they will invite us to become part of their communities—their families, clans, and tribes. They may mark this transition with a ritual of adoption into the group or initiation into the tribe. This is a mark of honor because it means the people trust us, but it also puts a new burden on us. Now we are insiders, and we must act as good insiders. If we are adopted as "uncles" or "aunts," we must act as good uncles and aunts. When our new "nieces" and "nephews" are married, we must bring appropriate gifts. When there is a family gathering, we must attend and help pay for the feast. If we do not, we will be viewed as a bad insider and our relationships with others will be strained. Being an insider helps us study intimate, private aspects of the culture. We are entrusted with the secrets of the people, but we must handle those secrets responsibly.

Some argue that our goal is ultimately to become total insiders—total participants, not observers. This, however, is neither possible nor desirable. While we want to identify with the people as much as possible, we can do this only as far as our Christian faith and conscience allow. Moreover, our value to the people is that we have knowledge and outside contacts that can help them. And if we are really insiders, we may become rivals for the social positions and resources in the community. Finally, entering fully into the world of the people makes multicultural translations and comparisons impossible.

Participant-observation adds a new dimension to research. We can observe a people as outsiders, using our own theories and categories. But when we study humans, we want to know what is going on in their minds, and this we can learn only by joining them in their daily lives. No longer are we studying impersonal objects—we are studying human beings who are like ourselves. Our theories must apply not only to other people but also to ourselves, since we, too, are humans. Furthermore, since we must treat the people we observe as rational, self-determining creatures like ourselves, we cannot use completely deterministic models to explain their behavior.

Finally, in studying people we must be aware that our very presence influences and affects them. If they do not think we are observing them (which is more likely if we have truly become participants), their actions may be more natural. If they think we are observing them (which happens when we remain outsiders, such as when pointing a camera) they will often "stage" their behavior. And we must remember that people have their own agendas and make decisions and act to achieve their own particular goals. In relating to us they may have their own purposes that shape the way they respond to us.

Conversations and Interviews

As we participate in the life of a community, occasions arise for us to talk with people about the questions we have. We can learn much from the ordinary, everyday conversations we have with people, wherever these take place.

Conversations can become interviews. The most informal of these are simply when we take note of what is said. We make no effort to control the direction of the conversation. In unstructured, but intentional, interviews we sit down with an informant and ask questions regarding a topic. We have no fixed set of questions to ask. Rather, new questions emerge as the conversation continues, and we are open to proceeding in new directions as information is gathered. In unstructured interviews it is generally best to begin with broad, open-ended questions and then ask narrower questions as one's knowledge of the topic grows. In studying people's activities, it is good to begin with the examination of objects, their uses, and the mechanics of the processes in which they are used. This type of interview is particularly important when we first begin to explore a subject.

In semiformal interviews we have a definite mental list of items we want to investigate (a protocol). As we ask our questions, we give the respondent considerable freedom to wander from the topic. But we also control the direction of the interview by drawing the discussion back to the basic research agenda.

In formal interviews we are intent on gathering specific kinds of data systematically. We have fixed questions that require specific answers. These questions may be essay questions to which the interviewee is free to give a long and detailed answer, or they may be more specific questions with a limited number of fixed answers.

Selecting a good informant for interviews is a delicate art and grows best out of the experiences of participant-observation. Through daily interaction the researcher sees which people are most involved in certain activities and what interests and "stakes" they have in them, thereby enabling the researcher to evaluate the accuracy of information given. The researcher must be cautious about drawing on people who may push themselves forward. These are often the marginal members of society who are looking for support and prestige. But those who are central to the society, able to understand the researcher's purpose, and willing to give information may be valuable interviewees.

Interviewing is useful not only in research but also in effective ministry. Any pastor, missionary, or leader must constantly monitor the congregation's thoughts and feelings, and this information is gathered largely by conversations and questioning. Learning the art of interviewing is essential to effective ministry. We must remember that this begins with a genuine relationship in which we are truly interested in the people, and only then moves to the gathering of data.

In interviewing we must assure the informants that we will keep their confidence and not use the information against them. In dealing with sensitive topics, it is better to discuss the material indirectly. Rather than asking, "What do *you* think or do?" ask "What do *others* (or people in another village) think or do?" Here are some tips: Avoid judgmental responses and learn to respond sensitively. Don't push the interview along. Wait quietly for the informant to continue. Let the informant know you are listening by affirmative statements such as, "Yes, I see." At appropriate times, share your own experiences.

In interviewing, remember that the answers people give reflect many things besides the question itself. People may tell you what they think you want to know in order not to offend you, or they may answer in order to get something from you for their own benefit. They may shape their answers to make themselves look good. Or they may provide made-up answers rather than admitting they have forgotten or don't know. It is important to evaluate responses for their accuracy and their deeper meanings.

Interviewing is an art, so practice it. Consciously evaluate an interview as it is going on, noting what blocks further discussion and what fosters trust. Remember that gestures, facial expressions, body language, and other subtle signs often speak louder than words.

Key Informants

When we want to know what "ordinary people" think, we need to talk to a number of them to get a general impression of their knowledge and opinions. The more people we interview, the more confident we are of the findings. But at this level we can make statements only about what "everyone" thinks.

Sometimes we want to study the knowledge systems of specialists. In this case, we select *key informants*, people the public believes are technical specialists in a given field. For example, we might interview the Hindu priests in a temple to learn about formal Hindu thought; a shaman to learn about folk religious beliefs concerning spirits, healing, and ecstatic religious experiences; a local historian to learn about the culture's past; or a local doctor to learn about traditional medicine systems. A key informant is someone in the society who, because of his or her experience and knowledge, is considered to be an expert in the subject that the ethnographer has chosen for research. Because of their expertise they are often leaders and decision makers in the society.

Choosing the right key informants is one of the most important and challenging aspects of cross-cultural ethnographic research. It is a delicate art that demands a great deal of time, patience, and energy. It is essential to establish a healthy, friendly, and open relationship with people who might become key informants.

Ethnosemantics

Ethnosemantics is the analysis of conceptual categories people use in thinking about reality. For example, each culture has words for colors, for geographic features, and for rituals such as marriage and death. Studying these words helps us understand how people view their world. Once the words used in a particular cultural domain are gathered, we can organize them into larger, more inclusive categories. And we can note how the categories relate to one another. For example, on an Indian road oxen, buffalo, humans, and sheep can be lumped as pedestrians. Motorized vehicles would include cars, buses, trucks, motor rickshaws, motorcycles, and mopeds. On the road, then, motorized vehicles of all types have priority over pedestrians of all types.[8] In this way, an examination of fundamental semantic categories can help us discover the worldview of a culture.

One way to begin studying the social structure of a community is to examine the kinship terms it uses. This can be done in various ways. The first is to study the terms people use when *referring to* particular relationships. We ask for the word a person uses to identify his or her father, mother, sister (older and younger), brother (older and younger), and so on. We can then explore what expectations the people have for each relationship.

---

8. For a fuller analysis of this particular situation, see Hiebert 1976.

This helps us to see how the people view relationships in a family or clan. For example, in many societies the same word is used when referring to a father and all the father's brothers. This shows that they view all these men as "fathers" who are part of a larger family and who are free to discipline their own children as well as one another's.

A second way to study kinship systems is to study the words people use when they *address* a relative. How do wives address their husbands, husbands their wives, daughters and sons their mother and father, and fathers and mothers their sons and daughters? This throws light on how participants view their relationships with others in their group. Respect and distance, familiarity and intimacy are often reflected in the words people use to address one another. In this way, ethnosemantic research can "unpack" the meanings associated with social categories in a culture.

CASE STUDIES

One of the most powerful methods of ethnographic research is the case study method. A case is any social event that has a beginning, a process, and an end. A biography is a case. It begins with the person's birth and ends with his or her death. A ritual, such as a Sunday morning service or a wedding, can be treated as a case. Legal disputes are also cases. They begin when the social order is disrupted by some misbehavior and end when the society finishes settling the matter.

One value of case studies is that we are looking at real-life events, not what people say should happen but what actually happens. Cases are particularly helpful in studying complex social phenomena because a variety of factors can converge in a single event. By analyzing these factors, we can learn a lot about the culture.

In gathering data on a case, it is best to use multiple sources of evidence. We can talk to the people involved, and to others outside the case, in order to gain different perspectives on it. This *triangulation* helps us both to check the facts of the case and to learn how different people explain what is going on.

The first level of analysis is *description*. Here our purpose is to explore and understand the facts involved in the event itself. If we study several similar cases, we begin to see patterns emerge that help us understand the processes involved. The second level of analysis moves beyond description to *explanation*. Here we generate hypotheses to explain what has happened in the case. These explanations may be historical—looking at the factors and processes leading up to the case; or these explanations may be synchronic—looking at the various factors and forces in the case and the relationship between them.

The strength of case studies is that they deal with real life in its everyday flow. They are not artificial situations. Moreover, they are not reductionist. They help us deal with the complexities of life by providing an open-ended research method and good qualitative data. Their limitation is that we cannot make broad generalizations based on the study of only a few cases. For this, quantitative studies such as surveys are needed.

Grounded Theory

In recent years another type of research strategy has emerged, one that is halfway between qualitative and quantitative research. Qualitative research seeks depth and richness in the data by studying a limited number of specific cases. It helps us to see humans in the complexities of their lives and to see the world as they see it. Quantitative research studies whole populations or samples of populations to test general human science theories. Grounded theory seeks to develop theories that emerge from the initial qualitative data and then are tested using quantitative data.[9] Anselm Strauss and Juliet Corbin define grounded theory as "*a general methodology* for developing theory that is grounded in data systematically gathered and analyzed. Theory evolves during actual research, and it does this through continuous interplay between analysis and data collection" (cited in Denzin and Lincoln 1998, 158). In other words, generating theory and doing research are two parts of the same process. Grounded theory is open to speculative thinking that goes outside the standard theories already in the literature. It is important, however, that the researcher be aware of literature relevant to his or her studies for purposes of comparison. It is difficult to generate good formal theory from just your own fieldwork.

Grounded theory seeks to develop dense, rich theory in the process of doing research. It avoids both the danger of simply giving descriptions of the data with little analysis and the danger of bringing in preformed theories that blind the researcher by focusing on a range of data that is too narrow. The latter danger overlooks the richness of human life, along with the deviations from main patterns that may open important doors to new theoretical insights. When the whole emphasis is on verifying previously

9. Grounded theory was introduced in 1967 by Barney Glaser and Anselm Strauss in *The Discovery of Grounded Theory*; see references cited at the end of this book.

established theory, there is no provision for discovering the unique perspectives that might change the theory. Barney Glaser and Strauss write:

> In verification, one feels too quickly that he has the theory and now must "check it out." When generation of theory is the aim, however, one is constantly alert to emergent perspectives that will change and help develop his theory. . . . The published word is not the final one, but only a pause in the never-ending process of generating theory. When verification is the main aim, publication of the study tends to give readers the impression that this is the last word. (Denzin and Lincoln 1998, 35)

Grounded theory begins by gathering facts, organizing categories, and only then formulating theories that can be later tested by quantitative means. Researchers gather data by observation, participant observation, interviews, and other qualitative methods. They seek to present the views of those studied, but they also take responsibility for interpreting what is observed, heard, or read in their own research-based frameworks.

Participatory Research and Action

In recent years a new approach called participatory research and action (PRA) has emerged for conducting human studies. In this approach the people being studied are invited to be involved as participants in a self-study project. Here the outside researcher helps the people define the topic to be studied, develop methods for gathering data, analyze the data, and draw conclusions. This method is powerful in cases where research is conducted to help people deal with specific problems, such as diseases, family unrest, and lack of food. If outside researchers come and decide what is wrong, decide on what must be done, and do the work, the projects generally fail because the people do not understand the remedies and have no ownership in the project. If they are involved in defining the problem from the outset, deciding on the solution, finding the resources, doing the job, and evaluating the outcome, then the project becomes theirs and they maintain it after the outsiders leave.

Human Rights

Finally, when we study humans we have a moral responsibility to protect them and their rights. Research provides information that can harm people. It is important, therefore, that we take steps to safeguard those we study.

One step is to ask people for permission to interview them and to explain the purposes of our research. Another is to keep their identities anonymous in our writing so that readers cannot trace the sources of our information. Often this is done by giving fictitious names to the people we interview.

Working closely with key informants for long periods of time raises the question of reciprocity. We gain much from the informants. In turn, we should expect to give something in return. One thing we must give is our friendship—to be available to spend time not only for gathering data, but also for fellowship and exchange. In most cultures it is appropriate to give key informants a gift. In a few cases it is appropriate to pay informants for the time they spend in working with us. Above all, we must remember that we are in relationships with people and must honor those relationships more than we honor our own goals.

Part 3

Mission as Intercultural Mediation

8

Missions as Glocal Mediation

The modern mission paradigm, developed roughly between 1700 and 1970, was characterized by "going" from one place to another to spread the gospel. Missionaries left Europe and North America to go to "the uttermost parts of the earth." The organizing principle was geography. Missionaries went to India, Africa, China, Latin America, Burma, the South Sea islands, and other parts of the world. They began along the coasts and then moved inland. They divided their work into geographic *fields* and brought the gospel to people who had never heard it. The flow was one way: from the West to the non-West; from the "civilized Christian world" to the "uncivilized pagan world." God used the modern mission movement, with all its flaws and failures, to plant churches around the world. Today, due in large measure to the sacrifices made by these missionaries, the young and vital churches and centers of Christianity are not in the West but in Africa, Korea, China, Latin America, India, and other lands once thought to be remote.

The world, too, has changed. In William Carey's day it took six months to reach India by sailing ship. In 1960 it took four weeks by steamship. Now we come and go in a day. In 1960 it took three weeks to send airmail letters and get a response. Now we have instant communication by telephone and

Portions of this chapter and the next one have already appeared in print under the title "The Missionary as Mediator of Global Theologizing" (Ott and Netland 2006, 288–308).

the Internet. We are rapidly becoming one global world in which events in one part of the world immediately affect the rest of the world.

As we have seen, in recent years scholars have turned their attention to the emergence of world systems. But studies show that most people still live in local and regional settings, even though they may venture from home from time to time. Out of these discussions have emerged theories of a *glocal* world in which different kinds of globalization interact in complex ways with regional and local systems.

There are many levels of cultural encounter in our postmodern and now emerging post-postmodern—or glocal—world. At the global level, cultures and nations around the world increasingly confront one another as travel, trade, global networks, and transnational organizations emerge. Within nations we are becoming increasingly aware of deep cultural differences as powerless communities increasingly find a voice in the public arena. Immigrant communities find social and cultural assimilation in their adopted lands full of tension and misunderstanding. Internally, these communities face additional generational differences that engender conflict and misunderstanding between parents and children.

In a glocal world full of tensions and conflicts, how can we work toward the unity of the church, theology, and mission? One way is to develop global systems from the top down: from centralized institutions built around specialists who define theology, organize the church, and manage missions. Another way is to develop global networks from the ground up: networks that begin at the local level and develop midlevel and global dialogues, partnerships, and networks for fellowship and ministry. From a free church perspective, it is the latter that we will explore here. The question is: how can we start with the many local and regional churches around the world and build a global fellowship—a fellowship that does ministry and theological reflection together without imposing these from above and that does not silence the weak but draws on the wisdom of those who are mature in faith?

It is important to remember that the missionary movement was one of the earliest forces creating global networks and new media of communication no less powerful than those established by the markets and information technology of the twentieth century. This was true of Catholic missions in the sixteenth and seventeenth centuries and even more so of Protestant missions of the eighteenth, nineteenth, and twentieth centuries. So the difficulties we face now are not really new ones.

Nevertheless the glocalization of the world and church has profound implications for missions in the twenty-first century, implications we have only begun to explore under the topics of truth, dialogue, religious plural-ism, relativism, contextualization, ecumenism, partnership, and local and global theologies. How should churches around the world relate to one another when there are great social, cultural, and theological differences as well as a desperate need to live together in peace? How do we respond to religious differences when we are committed to the truth of the gospel and the priesthood of all believers? What does globalization mean when it comes to evangelism and missions?

Mission as Mediation

What is the shape of the new mission paradigm emerging in the twenty-first century? A consensus has not yet emerged, but several points are increasingly clear. One is that missions to people who have yet to hear the gospel must continue. The number of people who have not heard the gospel meaningfully enough to make an intelligent response is greater now than when Bartholomäus Ziegenbalg and Heinrich Plütschau left for India in 1706. The task of pioneer missions is not finished. It is greater than ever.

A second fact is that a growing number of missionaries are *inbetweeners* who stand between different worlds, seeking to build bridges of under-standing, mediate relationships, and negotiate partnerships in ministry. In anthropological terms they are cultural mediators: those who stand between different communities and cultures. They need to know both well, and to speak on behalf of one to the other. Both communities will be suspicious of them because they do not know what the missionaries are doing when they are with the other group. But inbetweeners are increasingly vital to global missions and the global church. We now examine, first, some of the gulfs that need to be bridged in missions and then, second, some of the qualities missionaries who serve in this role must have in order to be effective in their ministries.

Between the Gospel and the World

The heart of missions has always been—and remains—the task of bridg-ing the gulf between the gospel and the world. In the past, it was assumed that the West had heard the gospel and that it was essentially Christianized. The rest of the world was assumed to be pagan and heathen. They were the ones who needed to hear the gospel for the first time.

Today the church is global, and the most vital churches are found in the non-West. Furthermore, parts of the West have returned to paganism. This has profoundly changed the way we perceive missions. First, the globalization of the church has made us much more aware that the gospel is a call to transform people, their societies, and their cultures, wherever they are. The West now is as much a mission field as the non-Western world. This raises questions of priority: how much effort should be put into reaching the West, where people already have an opportunity to hear the Good News, and how much should be given to the many parts of the world where people have no opportunity to hear it? The temptation is to lose sight of the big picture and to focus too much on the West, with its great spiritual needs, to the neglect of other parts of the world.

Second, globalization has made us even more aware of the need to contextualize the message, the mission, and the church in local societies and cultures. Contextualization of the gospel in local cultures began with using local languages, translating the Bible, and using local worship forms. There is an increasing awareness that evangelistic methods, too, need to be contextualized. And, questions arise about the contextualization of theology. Western theological categories cannot simply be translated into other languages and worldviews. Theological reflections in different cultures must be done initially in the people's own conceptual categories and then evaluated in the light of global theologizing. Moreover, we must link abstract, *experience-distant* concepts (which are often reductionist) with the concrete *experience-near* manifestations of theology in everyday life that are rich with practical implications.

These are profound questions related to the need for and limits to contextualization: To what extent can we use local signs, beliefs, and practices without losing the essence of the gospel and the church? How can we transform these local elements to become faithful communicators of the gospel? The dangers are to undercontextualize or to overcontextualize. The task calls for missionaries and leaders who understand both theology and human cultures well and can build bridges between them.

In order to be effective, missionaries must be incorporated into local social systems, a process known as indigenization:[1] what is the role of the missionary in the local society? *Missionary* is a role in the West, one that

---

1. To keep the social and cultural systems conceptually distinct, I use the word *indigenization* for the incorporation of the missionary and the church into the local *social* system. The "three selves," for instance, were matters of indigenization: economics (self-support), political-legal (self-governance), and societal reproduction (self-propagating). I use the term *contextualization* for the process of incarnating the gospel in local *cultural* systems.

is not found in other cultures. Local people look at the way missionaries behave and place them in one of their own cultural categories. Too often missionaries are seen by the people as rich landlords because they build large compounds, or as powerful patrons because they control resources and hire people, or as foreigners. How would they respond to the gospel if missionaries came as holy persons or servants or as transcultural mediators? What would a holy person or a servant look like in different cultures? How should transcultural mediators live locally? What would incarnational ministries look like in such cases?

Indigenization also has to do with the embodiment of the church in the local social system. Often this has been the hardest adjustment for Western missionaries to make. If they come from Episcopal churches, they set up episcopal styles of organization. If they come from American Protestant churches, they assume that democracy and elections are the best way to organize a church, even though these lead to polarization and lawsuits in many parts of the world. Missionaries rarely study the way local societies organize their communities—by elders, councils, chiefs, and others—and organize the local church accordingly.

It is becoming clear that all forms of ecclesiology are shaped by the societies in which they emerge, and they need both theological and social critique. How should the church deal with ethnic differences in the neighborhood and in the church—and the racism that so often emerges out of these? How should it deal with class and gender differences? What is its role in reconciliation and peace ministries in a conflict-torn world? Missions can no longer ignore the divisions and hostilities of societies.

Third, it is increasingly clear that missionaries must not only speak to the world for the church, but must also speak to the church for the world. Most local churches understand little about churches and cultures in other parts of the world. They assume that others should be like them. But missions must begin with truly loving others, and this requires a deep knowledge of them. Increasingly, missionaries must help sponsoring churches understand and identify with people in other places. Moreover, in every church there must be mission-minded leaders who constantly remind it of its missionary calling. Too often local churches are inwardly focused communities with their own subcultures. Through the process of institutionalization, they spend more and more of their efforts on building themselves up. Every church committee should have someone designated to speak for the world—to remind the church that some of its efforts should be focused on God's mission beyond the church walls.

Between Churches and Church

Another gulf that needs to be bridged is that between the local church and the worldwide church. In the past, mission churches were often supervised by sending churches. Today, they are increasingly mature, independent churches. Moreover, there has been rapid growth in locally initiated churches with few official ties to churches in other lands. There is a growing need for missionaries who build bridges of understanding and partnership among these diverse churches.

The emergence of relationships between local churches and global church structures, such as denominations and mission agencies, raises profound questions of power and control and of defining the essence of the gospel. It also raises difficult questions about the nature of partnership in mission. How can the gospel be presented in such a way that it is seen as belonging to the whole world, not simply one part of it? How can personnel, resources, and methods be used in pioneer work? How can cultural differences in multicultural teams be worked out in a way that enhances rather than undermines the work? Here missionaries are needed who can help mediate the deep differences between churches and individuals in the various parts of the world.

There are also questions about the essential nature of the global church. How can the church show the world that it is indeed one? In much of the world the dividedness of the church has been one of the great obstacles to its message. How can governance be truly shared? The global church needs missionaries from all countries—people who move between worlds and speak to the old churches for the young and to the young churches for the old. Only in this way can the global church be the united body of Christ.

Between Theology and Theologies

We have seen that reflection on the message of the gospel in local contexts is the central task of global missions. This raises the question of the relationship between the local theologies developed by churches in different cultures and theology as revealed in Scripture. How can we draw on the insights of local theologies and work toward a global understanding of the theological truths revealed in Scripture—truths given to humans in their cultural contexts as recorded in the Old and New Testaments, but truths that are universal in their application to all humans in their diverse contexts? Doing local theologies and mediating among them involves more than simply cultural issues. Ultimate truth is at stake, as is the underlying unity of the church.

To move from local theologies to an understanding of transcultural truths revealed in Scripture, we need a metatheology—theological reflection on how local theologies should be done. For us as evangelicals, this begins with the affirmation that Scripture is divine revelation and our final authority for the matters it addresses. All local theologies are our understanding of that revelation in our contexts and are vital, but not to be equated with Scripture.

An evangelical metatheology affirms that the interpretation of Scripture belongs to the church as a hermeneutical community. The church as hermeneutical community involves not only churches in different cultures and theological traditions today but also the historical church (Walls 1996). And, a metatheology must take seriously the leading of the Holy Spirit in the reading and interpretion of Scripture. It is only by God's Spirit that we are able to come to agreement at all, much less to base that agreement on the truth.

Between the Academy and the Mission Movement

Another chasm that needs to be bridged is that between missions as a movement and missiology as an academic discipline. In the future we will need missiologists who live between the academy and active missionary work. Increasingly we need careful research and reflection on the Word and on the world at large. Missions requires the best research and theoretical reflections to help guide us in an increasingly complex and confusing world. As such it must draw on the best that the academy can offer. So far the academy has been dominated by the West (Tiénou 1993). The growing voices of scholars from around the world have been largely ignored by mainstream theologians, often because Western scholars have not taken time to learn other languages well. Here missionaries and national scholars need to counter the hegemony of the Western academy, give voice to the theologies emerging in the young churches, and help build bridges of understanding and consensus among scholars around the world.

Between Changing World Systems

We are in a tremendous transition worldwide. Not only is the spread of global webs challenging societies, cultures, nation-states, and other local identities, but postmodernity is challenging the very foundations of the Enlightenment. Modernity and science are increasingly viewed as dominant metanarratives that oppress people and destroy the earth. Too often missionaries have been blind to their identification with their own nations and cultures, rather than with their citizenship in God's kingdom. They have failed to maintain a prophetic voice in their own societies. But what lies beyond the postmodernity that seeks to destroy the old tyranny? Will we fragment into a diversity that no longer understands human unity? Leaders are needed who are at home in both local and global settings and can affirm both local diversities and the oneness of humanity.

These leaders must also help Christians stand with confidence in contexts of pluralism and bear bold witness to Christ in a world seeking answers to questions about its very existence. Missionaries and transcultural leaders are essential to such a task, for it belongs to the whole church, not just the church in one part of the world. The problems are worldwide, and the global church must address them as faithful servants and witnesses to Christ. We are part of a movement that relates to real people and a real world, and as such we must never lose the biblical vision of God's saving love. That vision requires constant recommitment, sacrifice, and suffering.

The Ministry of Mediation

How can missionaries and missiologists live and minister as mediators? Our model is Jesus, who in his incarnation was fully God and fully human. He was equally at home as King of the universe on the throne in the palaces of heaven and as an infant in a manger in a cattle shed on earth. We can never begin to emulate him fully, but he provides us with a way of understanding our role in building bridges between different worlds.

Essential to developing global understanding and networks between churches and theologians is the process of intercultural mediation. Simply living between cultures does not make one a good mediator. What are some of the essentials for such a ministry?

Transcultural Analytical Frameworks

In the post-postmodern (Smith 1982; Laudan 1996) or glocal world, people must relate to one another because we increasingly live in one intertwined world, and we must do so recognizing the differences between us. To mediate between different peoples and cultures, we need a metacultural framework. Such a framework is not itself a culture. It is a grid that enables us to understand, translate, compare, and evaluate different cultures (fig. 8.1). In a sense, it is like a computer program that takes documents written in one format and translates them into another format.

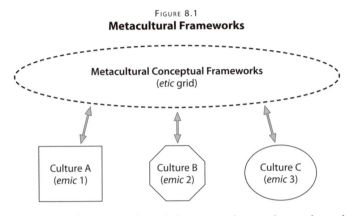

FIGURE 8.1
Metacultural Frameworks

There is no single metacultural framework. Anthropology has been working on such a grid from its inception. The early metacultural frameworks were essentially Western cultural grids. Taxonomies of different social, economic, political, and cultural systems were created using modern scientific categories. As the views of other peoples were taken seriously, those frameworks were rejected and newer ones developed. The current comparative frameworks are not entirely neutral either, but they are better than the earlier classifications and theories, just as modern translation theories are better than the old ones based on literal or Saussurian semiotics. It is important that all parties involved in mediation participate in the formation of such a grid.

Transcultural Mediators

To minister effectively as a mediator among different cultures, a person must become a transcultural person with a well-integrated metacultural identity. People who identify only with their own community will not be trusted by another. Those who seek to identify fully with another community and "go native" are viewed as frauds and rivals. We simply cannot fully identify with another culture in adulthood. In a sense, effective cultural mediators are outsider-insiders in any culture in which they find themselves. They seek to understand and empathize deeply with the people, but they know that ultimately they are still outsiders. It is this "outsiderness" that enables them to be bridges among different groups.

Outsiders are also able to bring people from different communities into dialogue with one another and to mediate that dialogue, seeking to help each community understand the others with the same sympathy they give to themselves. In interreligious witness, there must also be a move to go beyond simply understanding one another. Witness must be born to Christ as Lord. The goal of such dialogue is not simply peaceful coexistence, but a first step toward conversion to Christ. Still, in building relationships among Christians in different societies, effective mediators cannot side with either party. They must honestly and positively represent each side to the other, helping each to see the other's perspectives.

A number of characteristics mark the effective intercultural person. At a minimum, a transcultural person should be able "to communicate interpersonally; to adjust to various cultures; to develop interpersonal relationships; to deal with diverse societal systems; to understand another; and to manage psychological (intercultural) stress" (Cook 2005, 22). In a study of cross-cultural exchange programs, Bachner and Zeutschel (1994, 39) note that persons and parties involved in an exchange must meet three conditions:

1. The development of a transcultural frame of reference and identity whose norms transcend national and monocultural boundaries.
2. Relevant programmatic purposes and formal institutional expectations that exchanges [i.e., the mediators] are, in fact, to act as mediators.
3. Training that will prepare exchanges [the mediators] to assume a mediatory role and also confer legitimacy on formal status for them to do so.

The first task of cultural mediators is to help participants understand one another. The second is to mediate disagreements and conflicts. And the third is to bring about reconciliation where there are deep hatreds and memories of oppression (Volf, 1996). At the heart of intercultural mediation is love. Missionaries must truly love the people and identify with them in their common humanity. Only then can they bear bold witness to the gospel without arrogance or control.

9

Missionaries as Global Mediators

This inbetweenness
This walking the two
This expansiveness
That sees me neither
Fully one
Or the Other

Fully one
Seems to promise so much

Neither one
Seems so unfulfilled, empty, vague
. . . . .
The gift of betweenness
As we journey to be
Fully one

May we be generous with our
Discontent
      David Michie, Perth, Australia

David Michie, a young Australian Christian poet, captures the essence of this chapter, namely that missions in the twenty-first century will require new ways of relating to one another in a rapidly changing world. As we have seen, missionaries and global leaders must increasingly be transcultural mediators—people who live between cultures and deal with issues arising among different communities. In a glocal world the role of intercultural mediators becomes critical in maintaining relationships of cooperation and peace among the many locals who are increasingly being forced to interact with one another and with the larger global systems.

Our View of Others

At the heart of intercultural mediation is good intercultural relations based on true Christian love. As we saw in chapter 3, the foundation for such relationships is our perception of Others and "otherness." Too often in the past we have been shaped by the spirit of our time rather than the gospel. In the Age of Exploration, the West viewed Others as savages and as children; during the Enlightenment as pagans and primitives. These views privilege us with the power that comes from declaring ourselves to be the norm for humanity. But Christ rejects all earthly hierarchies by which we make ourselves superior to others. He calls us to be servants, not masters—servers, not served. Still we cannot follow the lead of post-moderns and view the Other as inscrutable either, for then there can be no deep relationship between us. So how should we view others? We must address the question of human differences and the sins of racism, classism, and genderism in the church.

Other Is Us

What, then, must we as Christians affirm about humans? The Scriptures lead us to a startling conclusion: *at the deepest level of our identity as humans there are no others—there is only us.* As Christians we must begin by affirming our common humanity with all people. On the surface we are male and female; black, brown, and white; rich and poor; old and young; but beneath these differences we are one humanity. The oneness of humanity is declared in the creation account (Gen. 1:26) and affirmed by the universalism implicit in the Old Testament (Ps. 148:11–13; Isa. 45:22; Mic. 4:1–2). "The entire history of Israel unveils the continuation of God's involvement with the nations. The God of Israel is the Creator and Lord of the whole world. For this reason Israel can comprehend its own history only in continuity with the history of the nations, not a separate history" (Bosch 1991, 18). The nations are waiting for Yahweh (Isa.

51:5). His glory will be revealed to all of them (Isa. 40:5). His servant is a light to the Gentiles (Isa. 49:6), and they will worship in God's temple in Jerusalem (Ps. 96:9).

In Christ and in the New Testament, the implications of our common humanity are worked out more fully. We see this first in Christ's teachings about the Other. An example of this is the parable of the Good Samaritan. When a Pharisee asked Jesus, "Who is my neighbor?" (in other words, "Who is one of us?"), Jesus turned the question on its head and asked, "If your Other—a Samaritan—is a neighbor to your brother, a suffering Jew, who are you to the Samaritan?" (paraphrased). The Pharisee was forced to admit either that he was indeed a neighbor to the Samaritan or that he had cut himself off from his fellow Jews. On another occasion Jesus said, "You have heard that it was said, 'You shall love your neighbor and hate your enemy,' but I say to you, 'Love your enemies and pray for those who persecute you'" (Matt. 54:43–44 NRSV). War demands that we hate our enemies and brand them as Others. But Jesus says that our enemies are us, therefore we must love them as our brothers and sisters, not oppress and kill them.

It is sin that divides and alienates us from one another. In the fall, humans were alienated from God (Gen. 3:8–10), men from women (Gen. 3:12, 16), brother from brother (Gen. 4:8, 23), and race from race (Gen. 11:9). Moreover, our common humanity extends beyond the fall. We are all sinners in need of redemption. Commenting on Luke's theology of mission, Bosch notes:

> Both the poor and the rich need salvation. At the same time, each person has his or her specific sinfulness and enslavement. The patterns of enslavement differ, which means that the specific sinfulness of the rich is different from that of the poor. . . . This means that the poor are sinners like everyone else, because ultimately sinfulness is rooted in the human heart. (1991, 104)

This commonality extends to the fact that Jesus died once for us all and to the fact that we are all potentially new creatures in Christ.

If we begin with the view that some people are Other, then all our attempts to build bridges of reconciliation between *us* and *them* will ultimately fail. Beneath the bridges we build, we will experience a chasm of otherness that will divide us when problems arise. If we begin by realizing that the Other is not Other but is Us, we start from biblical reality—from the fact that *we are one humanity*—regardless of how we feel about one another. Then we can celebrate our differences because they are secondary, because we know that no matter what misunderstandings and tensions may arise, underneath we have much in common. We can then begin the difficult task of bringing our mental images and social structures into line with that reality.

In affirming the oneness of humanity, we do not deny the great difficulty in understanding people in other cultures. It is easy to say that we love them when we have few deep relationships with them. Far too often we claim to know what others are thinking and feeling when, in fact, we are totally wrong. The more we study cultural differences, the more we realize how difficult it is to see others as humans like ourselves and to build deep interethnic relationships of mutuality and love. Nonetheless, we must put the time and energy into building such relationships and remember that despite differences, we have much in common.

Others Are Brothers and Sisters

Scripture leads us to a second startling conclusion: *in the church there are no others, there is only us—members of one body, brothers and sisters in faith*. Peter's amazement at what was taking place in the church can be detected in his words at the house of Cornelius: "I truly understand that God shows no partiality" (Acts 10:34 NRSV). The unity of the church is not an accidental by-product of the good news; it is an essential part of the gospel. For Paul, the gospel means announcing Christ's lordship over all reality and inviting all to submit to him. Paul's theme is "Jesus is Lord" (Rom. 10:9; 1 Cor. 12:3; Phil. 2:11). That theme—the reign of God present in Jesus Christ—has brought us all together under judgment and has, in the same act, brought us all together under grace.

In Christ we *are* one body (Eph. 4:4), one family. We do not need to invent the unity of the church. God has already established it. If we are not part of the body, we are not a part of Christ. What we need to do is to express that unity in our lives and in our churches. This unity is more basic than all human distinctions of ethnicity (Gal. 2:11–21), class (1 Cor. 10:1–11), and gender (Gal. 3:28; Acts 2:44–47; 4:32). Unity is not simply an abstract, spiritual principle. It must be lived in real human communities in which reconciliation between ethnic groups, classes, and genders is manifest. Bosch writes:

> Conversion does not pertain merely to an individual's act of conversion and commitment; it moves the believer into a community of believers and involves a real—even a radical—change in the life of the believer, which carries with

it moral responsibilities that distinguish Christians from "outsiders" while at the same time stressing their obligation to those "outsiders." (1991, 117)

But this is no ordinary family, no merely human community. In world religions, the gods demand the service of their worshipers, who must feed and clothe them, take them on processions, and offer sacrifices to them. In the church it is God who descends to identify himself with his creation, washes the feet of his disciples, offers himself as their sacrifice, and invites them to a banquet in which he himself is the meal! And when Christ returns in all his glory, he will seat his followers at his table and serve them (Luke 12:37). From a human perspective on power and glory, this is incomprehensible.

In the world we form clubs, corporations, and crowds, but these are not like Christian community. It is the true nature of the church to manifest *koinonia*. In *koinonia* the leaders are servants, the rich give their wealth to the poor, and the powerful empower the weak and oppressed. In short, the church's social order is an inverted hierarchy (Mark 10:35–37) in which serving ranks higher than being served (John 13:14–15) and ministering to others higher than being ministered to. In such a community, we have true oneness and fellowship.

Our Others' Keepers

The Scriptures lead us to a third startling conclusion: *we are our Others' keepers*. In Christ we are called to love and serve our fellow humans in need. This is the heart of Christian mission. We are not ministering to "infidels," "primitives," "pagans," or "natives." We are serving those who are created in God's image and called to be his saints. Our attitudes in ministry change when we see broken humans not simply as sinners but also as what God can make of them, potential saints in the kingdom, perfect and free.

This raises a difficult question: which is deeper—our identity as humans or our identity as Christians? If we see our deepest identity as Christians over against non-Christians, in missions we will always see ourselves as superior to the lost. We will see the expansion of Christianity in triumphalist terms as a conquest of the enemy.

In missions we must at the deepest level identify with people in our common humanity. We are all humans, part of creation over against the Creator. We are all formed in the image of God, fallen, and redeemable. Just as Christ identified with us in our humanity "while we were yet sinners," so we are called to identify with those who need salvation. Only then will we model an incarnational mission that really involves identification with the poor, oppressed, and lost. Only then will we avoid the arrogance and colonialism that have too often characterized our outreach. Bosch notes, "We are not the 'haves,' the *beati possidentes*, standing over against the spiritual 'have nots,' the *mass demnata*. We are all recipients of the same mercy, sharing in the same mystery" (1991, 484). We must minister with an attitude of humility because Christian faith is about grace that is freely given and the cross that judges us all.

Likewise, then, the church must refuse to understand itself as a sectarian society. It is actively engaged in a mission to those still outside the covenant community. To become a disciple means a decisive and irrevocable turning to both Christ and the Other. And yet the church is called not only to identify with the world but also to be a prophetic community inviting people to enter the kingdom of God. Berkhof writes, "The church can be missionary only if its being-in-the-world is, at the same time, a being-different-from-the-world" (trans. Bosch 1991, 386). This lies at the heart of mission. We cannot ignore the plight of our fellow humans, nor can we be content simply to sit and commiserate with them about our common condition. We share with them the good news of salvation and hope that was given to us, as we live together in a world lost in evil and despair.

A New Identity

In this world, we give high priority in our everyday lives to our primary reference group—to those who are "our kind of people." These primary reference groups tend to be based on ethnicity or nationalism. In postcolonial times, people have been increasingly willing to kill and die for ethnicity/nationalism. We must remember that our oneness with other humans is deeper than the identities that divide us on earth—ethnicity (Jew or Gentile), class (slave or free), and gender (male or female). These identities are not eternal. They are part of this passing age. As Christians, we have a new identity as children of God, which is eternal. In the church, at least, we should manifest this eternal reality and not be captive to our temporary worldly identities.

As mature Christians, we must know the oneness of humans and of Christians at the deepest level. But what about new converts? We cannot expect new believers to put their identity in Christ at the deepest level of their hierarchy of identities the moment they become Christians. This simply will not happen. Learning that being human and Christian are our deepest identities must be an intentional part of discipling. And it must be taught and modeled by those who are mature in faith. Similarly, new Christians must be helped to eliminate their racism and ethnocentrism, for it is sin. It divides the body of Christ, and it closes the door to effective witness to nonbelievers. Still, we must show the same patience and sympathy that we expect for ourselves in the sins that we are yet committing.

The matter is a serious one. If our deepest identities are ethnicity, culture, and nationalism, we can gather on the surface for worship, fellowship, and mission, but we know that when problems arise the underlying differences will emerge and we will divide. If, on the contrary, we are one at the deepest level of our identities, we can celebrate ethnic, cultural, and gender differences, knowing that when problems arise we will pull together as a body. Unity in the body of Christ does not rest on uniformity, but on our common "blood," which is the blood of Christ. We now are members of one family, and that identity cannot be taken from us, no matter how much we disagree or quarrel.

Unity in the church that breaks down walls of ethnicity, gender, and class is a sign of the kingdom of God now invading the earth. It takes place wherever Christ is Lord of our lives. As Karl Barth said, "[The church] exists . . . to set up in the world a new sign which is radically dissimilar to [the world's] own manner and which contradicts it in a way which is full of promise" (cited in Yancey 1995, 250). Philip Yancey adds:

> A society that welcomes people of all races and social classes, that is characterized by love and not polarization, that cares most for its weakest members, that stands for justice and righteousness in a world enamored with selfishness and decadence, a society in which members compete for the privilege of serving one another—this is what Jesus meant by the kingdom of God. (1995, 253)

As Christians, we must learn how to live out this reality in our everyday lives in a fallen world. In so doing, we show to the world the essence of the gospel.

Building Multicultural Relationships

How, in everyday life, can we learn to live as one with our Christian siblings when they are so different from us? Seeing others as humans created in the image of God and like us does not mean that building relationships with them is easy. We all know from personal experience that cultural differences can create a great many problems on our campuses, in our churches, and even in our homes. How can we understand and respond to these differences? In this book we have identified three basic dimensions to culture: ideas, feelings, and values. Each of these dimensions presents us with unique problems in intercultural relationships.

The Cognitive Dimension

Knowledge, ideas, beliefs, and worldviews are the conceptual content of a culture. That content provides people with linguistic categories with which to think, the logic they should use, and information about what exists and what does not. On the one hand, without this shared knowledge survival in life, communication with one another, and therefore community life are impossible. On the other hand, because shared knowledge provides us with the fundamental ingredients of our thoughts, we find it almost impossible to break away from its grasp.

The first barrier to relating well with people of another culture is *misunderstanding*. This has to do with a lack of knowledge about the other culture. Misunderstandings are often humorous and may have little serious consequences. We may extend our hand to someone from Japan, only to find that he or she is bowing graciously. We may set a time for an appointment, but the student appears a half hour later and does not offer an apology. In one case I know of, an African student arrived on campus at an American seminary for study. In the first weeks he formed a friendship with an American student, and when the American invited him to attend the funeral of his father, the African agreed to go. The day came and the African had to decide what clothes to wear. He decided he wanted to show deep appreciation for his new friend, so he dressed in ordinary work clothes so that, according to African custom, he could help in digging the grave. His primary concern was borrowing a shovel when he got there. When his American friend drove up dressed in a dark suit, the African realized there had been a misunderstanding.

Sometimes, however, misunderstandings can be shocking. Western missionaries to another country took along canned food. At first the people were friendly, but later they began to avoid the missionaries. The missionaries tried to find out why. Finally, one old man told them, "When you came, we watched your strange ways. You brought round tins and on the outside of some was a picture of beans. You opened them and inside were beans, and you ate them. On the outside of some were pictures of corn, and inside was corn and you ate it. On the outside of some were pictures of meat, and inside was meat, and you ate it. When you had your baby you brought more tins, and on the outside were pictures of babies. You opened them and fed the meat inside to your baby!" The people's conclusion was perfectly logical—but it was a misunderstanding.

Misunderstandings go deeper than misinterpreting ideas. Underlying our beliefs are worldviews of which we are hardly aware. These are the fundamental cognitive assumptions about the nature of things that we take for granted. For example, in many societies all rules and regulations are negotiable. Nothing is fixed forever. So when international students come to the United States to study, they automatically try to bend the rules through negotiation to get what they want. American professors, however, feel that to make exceptions is unfair to the other students and that these students are trying to manipulate them. And that makes them angry.

There are two types of misunderstandings that we need to overcome: our misunderstandings of people from other cultures and their misunderstandings of us. To overcome the first of these we must become learners and study the cultures of others. Here we must be careful not to jump to the conclusion that after a little effort we really do understand where people are coming from. For the most part, a culture makes sense to the people who participate in it, and when we think something they say or do is foolish we need to examine our assumptons more carefully.

To overcome others' misunderstandings of us and our customs, we need to be open and explicit in explaining our ways to them—and patient, not judgmental, with their misunderstandings. At times it is helpful to discuss how cultures differ in their way of handling things. This helps all those concerned see themselves and the unexamined assumptions they make.

The Affective Dimension

Culture also has to do with the feelings people have. And emotions play an important part in all human relationships, in our notions of etiquette and propriety, and in our ability to have fellowship.

Cross-cultural confusion at the affective level leads to ethnocentrism— the attitude that our own culture is better and more civilized than other cultures. This response has to do with feelings about other cultures, not with understanding them. We may well understand the situation and yet have a deep dislike for it. The root of ethnocentrism is our human tendency to respond to other people's ways by using our own affective assumptions and to reinforce these responses with deep feelings of approval or disapproval.

The problem is that when we are confronted by another culture, our own is called into question. This raises feelings of fear and anger. Our defense is to avoid the issue by concluding that our culture is better.

But ethnocentrism is a two-way street. We feel that people in other cultures are "primitive," and they judge us to be "uncivilized." For example, some North Americans were hosting a visiting Indian scholar at a restaurant. One of them who had never been abroad asked, "Do you really eat with your fingers in India?" Implicit in his question, of course, was his cultural attitude that eating with one's fingers is crude and dirty. North Americans use fingers for carrot sticks and potato chips, but never for mashed potatoes and gravy or T-bone steaks. The Indian scholar replied, "You know, in India we look at it differently than you do. I always wash my hands carefully before I eat, and I use only my right hand. And besides, my fingers have never been in anyone else's mouth. When I look at a fork or spoon, I often wonder how many other strangers have already had them in their mouths!" Such ethnocentrism occurs wherever cultural differences are found. North Americans are shocked when they see the poor of other cultures living in the streets. People in those societies are appalled when we surrender our aged and sick and the bodies of our departed to strangers for care.

The solution to ethnocentrism is empathy. We need to appreciate other cultures and their ways. But our feelings of superiority and our negative attitudes toward strange customs run deep and are not easily rooted out. In addition to learning about other cultures, and about the differences among cultures in general, we can overcome ethnocentrism by avoiding stereotyping and seeing other people as fully human individuals like ourselves. We need to remember and accept the fact that people love their own cultures. If we wish to reach them, we must learn to also love those cultures.

The Evaluative Dimension

Every culture also has values by which it judges human actions to be moral or immoral, proper or improper. Each also has its primary allegiances, its culturally defined goals, and its way of measuring success. Can things go wrong on the evaluative level? The answer is, "Yes." When we relate to other cultures, we tend to judge them before we have learned to understand or appreciate them. In so doing, we use the values of our own culture, not of metacultural or external criteria. Consequently, other cultures look less civilized to us.

Premature judgments are based on misunderstandings and ethnocentrism, so they are usually wrong. They also close the door to further understanding and communication. What is the solution? As we learn to understand and appreciate other cultures, we come to respect their integrity in organizing human life in viable ways. Some are stronger in one area, such as technology, and others in another area, such as family ties. But all "do the job," that is, they all make life possible and more or less meaningful.

This is not to take a position of cultural relativism. Cultures may be relative to one another, but all stand under the judgment of God's standards of righteousness and love that affirm the good in humanity and condemn the evil. We must judge the evil in all cultures. Not to do so would make us moral cretins. As Peter Berger notes, some acts, such as the Nazi gas chambers, are so evil that to refuse to condemn them in absolute terms would offer prima facia evidence "not only of a profound failure in the understanding of judgment, but more profoundly of a fatal impairment of *humanitas*" (1970, 66). In the end, cultural relativism leads to total disbelief in science, religion, and all systems of human knowledge. Ernest Gellner points out: "Relativism *does* entail nihilism: if standards are inherently and inescapably expressions of something called culture, and can be nothing else, then no culture can be subjected to a standard, because (*ex hypothesi*) there cannot be a trans-cultural standard which would stand in judgement over it" (1992, 50).

The problem is: How do we avoid judging other cultures by the standards of our own? How do we free ourselves from our monocultural biases? Interestingly enough, we cannot develop a transcultural perspective without first experiencing the shattering of our monocultural perspectives of truth and righteousness. When we first realize that other cultures have different norms, our temptation is to reject them without examination and to justify our own as biblical. This only closes the door for us to examine our own moral standards to determine which of them are based on biblical foundations and which on our cultural values.

Having experienced the shattering of our own cultural absolutes and faced the abyss of relativism, we can move beyond monoculturalism and relativism to an affirmation of the transcultural norms of Scripture and from there to the affirmation and critique of cultures. On the one hand, we will find that a great many norms in other cultures are good. For instance, in the non-Western world, a high value is often placed on taking time to relate, to care for the aged, and to share with the needy. On the other hand, in any culture we may find norms that conflict with biblical morality, such as self-centeredness, arrogance, manipulation, wife-beating, and idolatry.

Transcultural Persons

We have seen that persons and parties involved in intercultural mediation must develop a transcultural frame of reference and identity whose norms can transcend national and monocultural boundaries. Modernity claimed privileged truth that had to be taught to others. No mediation was required—only accurate communication. In the postmodern world, science has lost its privileged position and all belief systems are given equal place. But there is only "di-alogue," no mediation. We cannot be sure that we truly understand others, so we focus on ourselves. There is no real concern for others because they are inscrutable. In our day we need people who understand one another and can mediate between different worlds, whether these differences are based on culture, ethnicity, generation, or theological conviction.

To be glocal mediators, missionaries must belong to two or more worlds, not only in terms of lifestyle and beliefs, but at the deepest level of worldviews. Missionaries leave their home cultures where they are insiders and go to places where they are outsiders. As they live in the new society, they learn its customs and identify with it more deeply. They learn the language and begin to see the world as the people do. In so doing they become, to some extent, insiders. But they never fully become members of the culture. They are *outsider*-insiders. When the missionaries return to their home societies, they find that they no longer fully fit in there either. They now begin to see their own cultures as outsiders do. Again, they are *outsider*-insiders. In a sense they belong to two cultures; in a sense they do not belong fully to either.

This inner dividedness creates an identity crisis at the worldview level. One way to resolve this tension of identities is to affirm our original culture as our true identity and to go to other worlds as outsiders and visitors. We then think of sending our children "home" and of going there when we retire. We do not fully become transcultural people who can serve as intercultural mediators. A second answer is to seek to identify fully and completely with the other culture, or to "go native." But this is not only psychologically impossible, it is also destructive to our ability to build intercultural bridges. Ironically, those who seek to go native are sometimes not trusted by the local community. A third answer is to be cultural chameleons, to take on the trappings of the culture in which we find ourselves but have no true identity of our own. None of these options creates truly transcultural persons.

To become transcultural mediators we need transcultural identities. This requires developing a metacultural mental framework that enables us to live in different worlds while keeping our core identity secure. Such a framework emerges as we live in more than one culture and seek to understand each of them deeply from their own perspectives, while yet comparing and evaluating them. P. S. Adler notes that a multicultural person is:

> A person whose essential identity is inclusive of life patterns different from his own and who has psychologically and socially come to grips with a multiplicity of realities. Multicultural man is the person who is intellectually and emotionally committed to the fundamental unity of all human beings while at the same time he recognizes, legitimatizes, accepts and appreciates the fundamental differences that lie between people of different cultures. This new kind of man cannot be defined by the languages he speaks, the countries he has visited, or the number of international contacts he has made. Nor is he defined by his profession, his place of residence, or his cognitive sophistication. Instead, multicultural man is recognized by the configuration of his outlooks and worldview, by the way he incorporates the universe as a dynamically moving process, by the way he reflects on the interconnectedness of life in his thoughts and his actions, and by the way he remains open to the imminence of experience. (1977, 25)

A person with a multicultural identity such as this will be a good transcultural mediator.

Christian Love

We can learn to see others as us, tear down walls that divide us, build relationships of mutual understanding and respect, and become transcultural people—but without Christian love these are incomplete. Christian love is to be unconditionally committed to those we meet, including our enemies. As mediators we must be other-centered and love those we serve.

As fallen humans we love ourselves. When we are with others, we love to talk about ourselves and our experiences, show our pictures, and demonstrate our skills. When we run out of things to say, we move on to find other audiences. When conversations turn to others and their stories, we are soon disinterested. To love is to focus attention on the persons around us. It is to ask them questions about themselves in order to truly learn to know them. It is to affirm their personhood and the gifts God has given them. And it is to invite them to come to know Jesus Christ, too, within their cultural contexts, just as we ourselves, by God's grace, have done. Such Christian love is the central element in the work of missions. Without it, all of our best efforts are in vain.

References Cited

Adler, P. S. 1977. "Beyond Cultural Identity: Reflections upon Cultural and Multicultural Man." In *Culture Learning: Concepts, Applications, and Research*, ed. R. Brislin, 24–41. Honolulu: East-West Center.

Anderson, David. 1985. "The Rubicon of Involvement: Social Work and Anthropology." In *Advocacy and Anthropology: First Encounters*, ed. Robert Paine, 149. St. Johns: Institute of Social and Economic Research.

Appadurai, Arjun. 1996. *Modernity at Large: Cultural Dimensions of Globalization*. Minneapolis: University of Minnesota Press.

Arber, Edward. 1885. *The First Three English Books on America (1511–1555)*. Edinburgh: Turnbull and Spears.

Bachner, D. J., and U. Zeutschel. 1994. *Utilizing the Effects of Youth Exchange: A Study of the Subsequent Lives of German and American High School Exchange Participants*. New York: Council on International Educational Exchange.

Barbour, Ian. 1974. *Myths, Models, and Paradigm: A Comparative Study in Science and Religion*. New York: Harper and Row.

Barnard, Alan. 2000. *History and Theory in Anthropology*. Cambridge: Cambridge University Press.

Barrett, David B., et al. 2001. *World Christian Encyclopedia*. Oxford: Oxford University Press.

Bateson, Gregory. 1972. *Steps to an Ecology of Mind*. New York: Chandler.

Bellah, Robert, et al. 1985. *Habits of the Heart: Individualism and Commitment in American Life*. Los Angeles: University of California Press.

Berger, P. L. 1970. *The Sacred Canopy*. Garden City, NY: Doubleday.

Berger, P. L., and T. Luckman. 1966. *The Social Construction of Reality: A Treatise in the Sociology of Knowledge*. Garden City, NY: Doubleday.

Berger, P. L., Brigitte Berger, and Hansfried Kellner. 1973. *The Homeless Mind: Modernization and Consciousness*. New York: Irvington Publishers.

Berger, Peter, and Samuel Huntington. 2003. *Many Globalizations: Cultural Diversity in the Contemporary World*. Oxford: Oxford University Press.

Berlin, Brent, and Paul Kay. 1969. *Basic Color Terms: Their Universality and Evolution*. Berkeley: University of California Press.

Bodanis, David. 2000. $E = mc^2$: *A Biography of the World's Most Famous Formula*. New York: Berkeley Publishing Group.

Bosch, David. 1991. *Transforming Missions: Paradigm Shifts in Theology of Mission*. Maryknoll, NY: Orbis Books.

Brody, Howard, and David S. Sobel. 1979. "A Systems View of Health and Disease." Chapter 4 in *Ways of Health: Holistic Approaches to Ancient and Contemporary Medicine*, ed. David S. Sobel. New York: Harcourt.

Buckser, Andrew, and Stephen D. Glazier, eds. 2003. *The Anthropology of Conversion*. Lanham, MD: Rowman and Littlefield Publishers.

Cassidy, Vincent. 1968. *The Sea around Them, A.D. 1250*. Baton Rouge: Louisiana State University Press.

Chambers, Robert. 1997. *Whose Reality Counts? Putting the First Last*. London: Intermediate Technology.

Clifford, James, and George E. Marcus, eds. 1986. *Writing Culture: The Poetics and Politics of Ethnography*. Berkeley: University of California Press.

Codrington, R. H. 1891. *The Melanesians: Studies in Their Anthropology and Folklore*. Oxford: Clarendon Press.

Cohen, Robin. 1997. *Global Diasporas: An Introduction*. London: UCL Press.

Conklin, Harold C. 1955. "Hamuno Color Categories." *Southwestern Journal of Anthropology* 11:339–44.

Conrad, Joseph. 1950. *Heart of Darkness*. New York: Signet. (Orig. pub. 1890.)

Cook, Charles. 2005. "Assessing the Long-Term Impact of Intercultural Sojourners: Contributions of the CBC Intercultural Sojourners to Developing and Global Perspective." PhD diss., Trinity International University.

Crush, Jonathan, and David McDonald. 2000. "Transnationalism, African Immigration, and New Migrant Spaces in South Africa." *Canadian Journal of African Studies* 34:1–19.

Cvetkovich, Ann, and Douglas Kellner. 1997. *Articulating the Global and the Local: Globalization and Cultural Studies*. Boulder, CO: Westview.

D'Andrade, R. G., E. A. Hammel, D. Adkins, and C. M. McDaniel. 1975. "Academic Opportunity in Anthropology: 1974–90." *American Anthropologist* 77:753–73.

Defoe, Daniel. 1961. *Robinson Crusoe*. New York: Doubleday. (Orig. pub. 1719.)

Dennis, James. 1897–1906. *Christian Missions and Social Progress*. 3 vols. Edinburgh: Oliphant, Anderson and Ferrier.

Denzin, Norman, and Yvonna S. Lincoln. 1998. *The Qualitative Inquiry Reader*. Thousand Oaks, CA: Sage Publications.

Devereux, George. 1967. *From Anxiety to Method in Behavioral Sciences*. The Hague: Mouton.

Douglas, Mary. 1966. *Purity and Danger: An Analysis of Concepts of Pollution and Taboo*. London: Routledge and Kegan Paul.

———. 1969. *Natural Symbols: Explorations in Cosmology*. London: Routledge and Kegan Paul.

———. 1982. "Introduction to Grid/Group Analysis." In *Essays in Sociology of Perception*, ed. Mary Douglas, 1–8. London: Routledge and Kegan Paul.

Ebeling, Gerhard. 1963. "The Meaning of Biblical Theology." In *Word and Faith*. London: SCM Press.

———. 1973. *Introduction to a Theological Theory of Language*. London: Collins.

Elliott, J. H. 1970. *The Old World and the New: 1492–1650*. Cambridge: Cambridge University Press.

Ellul, Jacques. 1964. *The Technological Society*. New York: Random House.

———. 1967. *The Presence of the Kingdom*. New York: Seabury.

———. 1986. *Subversion of Christianity*. Grand Rapids: Eerdmans.

Elwood, Douglas J. 1978. *What Asian Christians Are Thinking*. Quezon City, Philippines: New Day.

————. 1980. *Asian Christian Theology: Emerging Themes*. Philadelphia: Westminster.

Erickson, Millard. 1998. *Christian Theology*. Grand Rapids: Baker Academic.

Escobar, Arturo. 1995. *Encountering Development: The Making and Unmasking of the Third World*. Princeton, NJ: Princeton University Press.

Evans, G. R., A. E. McGrath, and A. D. Gallway. 1986. *The Science of Theology*. Grand Rapids: Eerdmans.

Fabian, Johannes. 1983. *Time and the Other: How Anthropology Makes Its Object*. New York: Columbia University Press.

Ferguson, James. 1997. "Anthropology and Its Evil Twin: 'Development' in the Constitution of a Discipline." In *International Development and the Social Sciences*, ed. F. Cooper and R. Packard, 150–75. Berkeley: University of California Press.

Finger, Thomas N. 1985. *Christian Theology: An Eschatological Approach*. Vol. 1. Scottdale, PA: Herald Press.

Fisher, Walter R. 1987. *Human Communication and Narrative: Toward a Philosophy of Reason, Values, and Action*. Colombia: University of South Carolina.

Frake, Charles O. 1961. "The Diagnosis of Disease among the Subanun of Mindanao." *American Anthropologists* 63:113–32.

Fredrickson, George M. 2002. *Racism: A Short History*. Princeton, NJ: Princeton University Press.

Friedman, Thomas. 2000. *The Lexus and the Olive Tree*. New York: Farrar, Straus and Giroux.

Frykenberg, Robert E. 1996. *History and Belief: The Foundations of Historical Understanding*. Grand Rapids: Eerdmans.

Fuller, Daniel P. 1997. "Biblical Theology and the Analogy of Faith." *International Journal of Frontier Missions* 14:65–74.

Gannon, Martin J. 2007. *Paradoxes of Culture and Globalization*. Thousand Oaks, CA: Sage Publications.

Geertz, Clifford. 1973. *The Interpretation of Cultures: Selected Essays*. New York: Basic Books.

————. 1983. *Local Knowledge: Further Essays on Interpretive Anthropology*. New York: Basic Books.

———. 1988. *Works and Lives: The Anthropologist as Author*. Stanford, CA: Stanford University Press.

Gellner, Ernest. 1992. *Postmodernism, Reason, and Religion*. London: Routledge.

Giddens, Anthony, et al. 2003. *Introduction to Sociology*. New York: W. W. Norton.

Glaser, Barney G., and Anselm Strauss. 1967. *The Discovery of Grounded Theory: Strategies for Qualitative Research*. Edison, NJ: Aldine Transaction.

Grunbaum, A. 1957. "Complementarity in Quantum Physics and Its Philosophical Generalizations." *Journal of Philosophy* 54:713–27.

Habermas, Jürgen. 1971. *Knowledge and Human Interests*. Boston: Beacon.

Haleblian, Krikor G. 2004. "Art, Theology, and Contextualization: The Armenian Orthodox Experience." *Missiology: An International Review* 32:309–35.

Harries-Jones, Peter. 1985. "From Cultural Translator to Advocate: Changing Circles of Interpretation." In *Advocacy and Anthropology: First Encounters*, ed. Robert Paine. St. Johns: Institute of Social and Economic Research.

Harris, Marvin. 1968. *The Rise of Anthropological Theory*. New York: Thomas Y. Crowell Co.

Harvey, David. 1989. *The Condition of Postmodernity*. Cambridge, MA: Blackwell.

Hauerwas, Stanley, and William Willimon. 1989. *Resident Aliens: Life in the Christian Colony*. 2nd ed. Nashville: Abingdon.

Hayakawa, S. I. 1991. *Language in Thought and Action*. Orlando, FL: Harcourt.

Herzfeld, Michael. 2001. *Anthropology: Theoretical Practice in Culture and Society*. Oxford: Blackwell Publishers.

Hiebert, Paul G. 1976. "Traffic Patterns in Seattle and Hyderabad: Immediate and Mediate Transactions." *Journal of Anthropological Research* 32 (1976): 326–33.

———. 1982. "The Flaw of the Excluded Middle." *Missiology* 10.1:35–47.

———. 1989. "Form and Meaning in the Contextualization of the Gospel." In *The Word among Us*, ed. Dean S. Gilliland, 101–20. Dallas: Word.

———. 1994. *Anthropological Reflections on Missiological Issues*. Grand Rapids: Baker Academic.

———. 1996. "The Social Sciences and Missions: Applying the Message." In *Missiology and the Social Sciences: Contributions, Cautions, and Conclusions*, ed. Edward Rommen and Gary Corwin. EMS 4. Pasadena, CA: William Carey Library.

———. 1999. *Missiological Implications of Epistemological Shifts*. Harrisburg, PA: Trinity Press.

———. 2006a. "Missional Theology." *Missiology* 31.2:219–38.

———. 2006b. "The Missionary as Mediator of Global Theologizing." In *Globalizing Theology: Belief and Practice in an Era of World Christianity*, ed. Craig Ott and Harold A. Netland, 288–308. Grand Rapids: Baker Academic.

———. 2007. "Western Images of Others and Otherness." In *This Side of Heaven: Race, Ethnicity, and Christian Faith*, ed. Robert J. Priest and Alvaro Nieves, 97–110. New York: Oxford University Press.

———. 2008. *Tranforming Worldviews*. Grand Rapids: Baker Academic.

Hiebert, Paul, and Frances F. Hiebert, eds. 1987. *Case Studies in Missions*. Grand Rapids: Baker Academic.

Hiebert, Paul, and Tite Tiénou. 2006. "Missional Theology." *Missiology* 34.2:221–38.

Hiebert, Paul, Daniel Shaw, and Tite Tiénou. 1999. *Understanding Folk Religion: A Christian Response to Popular Beliefs and Practices*. Grand Rapids: Baker Academic.

Hnaff, Marcel. 1998. *Claude Levi-Strauss and the Making of Structural Anthropology*. Translated by Mary Baker. Minneapolis: University of Minnesota Press.

Horowitz, Donald L. 1985. *Ethnic Groups in Conflict*. Berkeley and Los Angeles: University of California Press.

Horton, Robin. 1967. "African Traditional Thought and Western Science I & II." *Africa* 37:50–155.

Hunn, Eugene. 1982. "Utilitarian Factor in Folk Biological Classification." *American Anthropologist* 94:830–47.

Hunsberger, George R., and Craig Van Gelder, eds. 1996. *The Church between Gospel and Culture: The Emerging Mission in North America*. Grand Rapids: Eerdmans.

Huntington, Samuel P. 1996. *The Clash of Civilizations and the Remaking of World Order.* New York: Simon and Schuster.

Inda, Jonathan Xavier, and Renato Rosaldo, eds. 2007. *The Anthropology of Globalization: A Reader.* Oxford: Blackwell.

Jarvie, I. C. 1975. "Epistle to the Anthropologists." *American Anthropologist* 77:253–66.

Jayakarn, Ravi. 2003. *Participatory Poverty Alleviation and Development: A Comprehensive Manual for Development Professionals.* Hong Kong: World Vision China.

Jeffrey, David L. 1980. "Medieval Monsters." In *Manlike Monsters on Trial,* ed. Marjorie Halpin and Michael Ames. Vancouver: University of British Columbia Press.

Johnstone, Patrick. 2000. *Operation World.* Carlisle, UK: Paternoster.

Jones, E. S. 1925. *The Christ of the Indian Road.* New York: Abingdon.

Kahn, Joel S. 1980. *Minangkabau Social Formations: Indonesian Peasants and the World Economy.* Cambridge: Cambridge University Press.

Kirk, J. Andrew, and Kevin J. Vanhoozer, eds. 1999. *To Stake a Claim: Mission and the Western Crisis of Knowledge.* Maryknoll, NY: Orbis Books.

Korbzybski, Alfred. 1933. *Sense and Sanity: An Introduction to Non-Aristotelian Systems and General Semiotics.* International Non-Aristotelian Library Publishing.

Kuhn, Thomas S. 1970. *The Structure of Scientific Revolution.* Chicago: University of Chicago Press.

Kuper, Adam. 1974. *Anthropologists and Anthropology.* New York: Pica.

Las Casas, Bortholome de. 1971. *A Selection of His Writings.* Edited and translated by G. Sanderlin. New York: Knopf.

Laudan, Larry. 1977. *Progress and Its Problems: Towards a Theory of Scientific Growth.* Berkeley: University of California Press.

———. 1996. *Beyond Positivism and Relativism: Theory, Method, and Evidence.* Boulder: Westview.

Lee, Mangaung. 1978. "A Post Critical Reading of the Bible as a Religious Text." *Asia Journal of Theology* 14:272–85.

Levi, Edward H. 1949. *An Introduction to Legal Reasoning.* Chicago: University of Chicago Press.

Levy-Bruhl, Lucien. 1966. *The Soul of the Primitive*. New York: Praeger. (Orig. pub. 1928.)

Lewellen, Ted C. 2002. *The Anthropology of Globalization: Cultural Anthropology Enters the 21st Century*. Westport, CT: Bergin and Garvey.

Lewis, C. S. 1961. *Preface to Paradise Lost*. New York: Oxford University Press.

Lingenfelter, Sherwood. 1996. *Agents of Transformation: A Guide for Effective Cross-Cultural Ministry*. Grand Rapids: Baker Academic.

———. 1998. *Transforming Culture: A Challenge for Christian Mission*. 2nd ed. Grand Rapids: Baker Academic.

Loewen, Jacob. 1992. "What Is Happening in Anthropology? An Example for Missionaries and Mission Boards." *Mission Focus* 20.3:47–50.

Lovejoy, Arthur. 1936. *The Great Chain of Being: A Study of the History of an Idea*. Cambridge, MA: Harvard University Press.

Lumeya, Nzash. 1988. "Curse of Ham's Descendants: Impact on Zairian Mbala Mennonite Brethren." PhD diss., Fuller Theological Seminary.

Luria, A. R. 1976. *Cognitive Development: Its Cultural and Social Foundations*. Cambridge, MA: Harvard University Press.

Luzbetak, Louis. 1988. *The Church and Cultures*. Maryknoll, NY: Orbis.

Lyons, John. 1977. *Semantics*. Vol. 1. Cambridge: Cambridge University Press.

Lyotard, Jean-Francois. 1984. *The Postmodern Condition: A Report on Knowledge*. Minneapolis: University of Minnesota Press.

MacKay, D. M. 1974. "Complementarity in Scientific and Theological Thinking." *Zygon* 9:225–44.

Malik, Charles. 1987. *A Christian Critique of the University*. 2nd ed. Waterloo, ON: North Waterloo Academic Press.

Malina, Bruce. 1986. *Christian Origins and Cultural Anthropology: Practical Models for Biblical Interpretation*. Atlanta: John Knox.

Manuel, Frank. 1959. *The Eighteenth Century Confronts the Gods*. Cambridge, MA: Harvard University Press.

Marcus, George E., and James Clifford. 1985. "The Making of Ethnographic Texts: A Preliminary Report." *Current Anthropology* 26:267–71.

Marcus, George E., and Michael M. J. Fisher. 1986. *Anthropology as Cultural Critique: An Experimental Monument in Human Sciences.* Chicago: University of Chicago Press.

Maybury-Lewis, David. 1985. "Brazilians, Indianist Policy: Some Lessons from the Shavante Project." In *Native Peoples and Economic Development: Six Case Studies from Latin America*, ed. Theodore Macdonald Jr. Cultural Survival Occasional Paper No. 16. Cambridge, MA.

McFague, Sallie. 1982. *Metaphorical Theology: Models of God in Religious Language.* Philadelphia: Fortress.

McGrane, Bernard. 1989. *Beyond Anthropology: Society and the Other.* New York: Columbia University Press.

McGrath, Alister E. 1998. *Historical Theology: An Introduction to the History of Christian Thought.* Oxford: Blackwell.

Melville, Herman. 1974. *Typee.* New York: Airmont. (Orig. pub. 1846.)

Miller, Jay. 1982. "Matters of the (Thoughtful) Heart: Focality or Overlap." *Journal of Anthropological Research* 38:274–87.

Montefiore, Hugh, ed. 1992. *The Gospel and Contemporary Culture.* London: Mowbray.

Morrison, John. 2004. "Barth, Barthians, and Evangelicals: Reassessing the Question of the Relationship of Holy Scripture and the Word of God." *Trinity Journal* 25:187–213.

Neill, Stephen. 1982. *A History of Christian Missions.* Harmondsworth, Middlesex, England: Penguin Books.

Newbigin, Lesslie. 1966. *Honest Religion for Secular Man.* London: SCM Press.

———. 1986. *Foolishness to the Greeks: The Gospel and Western Culture.* Grand Rapids: Eerdmans.

———. 1989. *The Gospel in a Pluralist Society.* Grand Rapids: Eerdmans.

Orwell, George Marrakech. 1954. *A Collection of Essays.* New York: Doubleday.

———. 1956. *The Orwell Reader.* San Francisco: Harcourt, Brace, Jovanovich.

Ott, Craig, and Harold A. Netland, eds. 2006. *Globalizing Theology: Belief and Practice in an Era of World Christianity.* Grand Rapids: Baker Academic.

Paine, Robert, ed. 1985. *Advocacy and Anthropology: First Encounters.* St. Johns, NF: Institute of Social and Economic Research.

Pannenberg, Wolfhart, et al., eds. 1968. *Revelation as History: A Proposal for a More Open, Less Authoritarian View of an Important Theological Concept.* New York: Macmillan.

Parsons, Talcott, and Edward Shills, eds. 1952. *Toward a General Theory of Action.* Cambridge, MA: Harvard University Press.

Peirce, Charles S. 1955. *Philosophical Writings of Peirce.* Edited by Justus Buchler. New York: Dover Publications.

———. 1958. *Charles S. Peirce: Selected Writings.* New York: Dover Publications.

Peterson, Eugene. 1974. *Subversive Spirituality.* Grand Rapids: Eerdmans.

———. 1997. *Leap Over a Wall: Earthy Spirituality for Everyday Christians.* San Francisco: HarperSanFrancisco.

Petty, William. 1927. *The Petty Papers.* Edited by Marquess of Lansdowne. London: Fairfield. (Orig. pub. 1677.)

Piaget, Jean. 1966. *The Origins of Intelligence in the Child.* London: Routledge and Kegan Paul.

Pobee, John. 1982. "Political Theology in the African Context." *African Theological Journal* 11:168–72.

Polanyi, Michael. 1974. *Personal Knowledge.* Chicago: University of Chicago Press.

Rader, William. 1978. *The Church and Racial Hostility: A History of Interpretation of Ephesians 2:11–12.* Tübingen: Mohr.

Ramachandra, Vinoth. 1999. *Faiths in Conflict: Christian Integrity in a Multicultural World.* Secunderabad, India: OM Books.

Reining, Conrad C. 1970. "A Lost Period of Applied Anthropology." In *Applied Anthropology: Readings in the Uses of the Science of Man,* ed. James A. Clifton, 3–11. Boston: Houghton Mifflin.

Ricoeur, Paul. 1981. *Hermeneutics and the Human Sciences: Essays on Language, Action, and Interpretation.* Edited by John B. Thompson. Cambridge: Cambridge University Press.

Rogge, A. E. 1976. "A Look at Academic Anthropology: Through a Graph Darkly." *American Anthropologist* 78:829–43.

Romantz, David S., and Kathleen Elliott Vinson. 1998. *Legal Analysis: The Fundamental Skill.* Durham, NC: Carolina Academic Press.

Said, Edward W. 1995. *Orientalism: Western Conceptions of the Orient.* London: Penguin Books. (Orig. pub. 1978.)

Salamone, Frank. 1986. "Missionaries and Anthropologists: An Inquiry into the Ambivalent Relationship." *Missiology* 14:55–70.

Sanneh, Lamin. 1993. *Encountering the West: Christianity and the Global Cultural Process*. Maryknoll, NY: Orbis Books.

Saussure, Ferdinand de. 1916. *Cours de Linguistiques General*. Paris. Translation: *Course in General Linguistics*. Edited by Charles Bally and Albert Sechehaye. New York: McGraw-Hill.

Schneider, Robert J. 1985. *Constructing Local Theologies*. Maryknoll, NY: Orbis Books.

Schultz, Donald L. 1989. *Developing an Asian Evangelical Theology*. Mandalujyong, Metro Manila: Barro.

Shenk, Wilbert. 1980. "The Changing Role of the Missionary: From 'Civilization to Contextualization.'" In *Missions, Evangelism, and Church Growth*, ed. C. Norman Kraus, 33–58. Scottdale, PA: Herald Press.

Smith, Huston. 1982. *Beyond the Post-Modern Mind*. Wheaton: Quest Books.

Stanley, Brian. 2001. "Christian Missions and the Enlightenment: A Re-evaluation." In *Christian Missions and the Enlightenment*, ed. Brian Stanley, 1–21. Grand Rapids: Eerdmans.

Stott, John R. W. 1979. *The Message of Ephesians*. Downers Grove, IL: InterVarsity.

Taber, Charles R. 1978. "Is There More Than One Way to Do Theology? Anthropological Comments on the Doing of Theology." *Gospel in Context* 1:4–10.

———. 1991. *The World Is Too Much with Us: "Culture" in Modern Protestant Missions*. Macon, GA: Mercer University Press.

Tiénou, Tite. 1990. *The Theological Task of the Church in Africa*. 2nd ed. Achimota, Ghana: Africa Christian Press.

———. 1993. "Forming Indigenous Theologies." In *Toward the 21st Century in Christian Mission*, ed. James M. Phillips and Robert T. Cootie, 245–52. Grand Rapids: Eerdmans.

Todorov, Tzvetan. 1984. *The Conquest of America: The Question of the Other*. New York: Harper and Row.

Turner, Harold. 1981. "Religious Movements in Primal (or Tribal) Societies." *Mission Focus* 9:45–54.

Turner, Victor 1967. *The Forest of Symbols: Aspects of Ndembu Ritual*. Ithaca, NY: Cornell University Press.

————. 1977. *The Ritual Process*. Ithaca, NY: Cornell University Press.

Tyler, Stephen. 1986. "Post-Modern Ethnography: From Document of the Occult to Occult Document." In *Writing Culture: The Poetics and Politics of Ethnography*, ed. James Clifford and George E. Marcus. Berkeley: University of California.

Van Engen, Charles. 1997. "Mission Theology in the Light of Postmodern Critique." *International Review of Mission* 86:437–61.

Volf, Miroslav. 1996. *Exclusion and Embrace: A Theological Exploration of Identity, Otherness, and Reconciliation*. Nashville: Abingdon.

Von Bertalanffy, Ludwig. 1981. *General System Theory: Foundations, Development, Applications*. New York: George Braziller.

Vos, Gerhardus. 1948. *Biblical Theology*. Grand Rapids: Eerdmans.

Wainwright, Geoffrey. 1980. *Doxology: The Praise of God in Worship, Doctrine, and Life: A Systematic Theology*. New York: Oxford University Press.

Wallace, A. F. C. 1958. "Revitalization Movements." *American Anthropologist* 58:264–81.

Wallerstein, Immanuel. 1974. *The Modern World-System: Capitalist Agriculture and the Origins of the European World-Economy in the Sixteenth Century*. New York: Academic Press.

Walls, Andrew. 1996. *The Missionary Movement in Christian History*. Maryknoll, NY: Orbis Books.

————. 2002. *The Cross-Cultural Process in Christian History*. Maryknoll, NY: Orbis Books.

Whitehead, Alfred North. 1938. *Modes of Thought*. New York: Free Press.

Wiebe, Donald. 1976. "Explanation and the Scientific Study of Religion." *Zygon* 11:35–49.

Wilk, Stan. 1977. "Castaneda: Coming of Age in Sonora." *American Anthropologist* 79:84–91.

Wilson, Bryan, ed. 1970. *Rationality*. New York: Harper and Row.

Wink, Walter. 1992. *Engaging the Powers: Discernment and Resistance in a World of Domination*. Minneapolis: Fortress.

Wolf, Eric R. 1982. *Europe and the People without History*. Berkeley: University of California Press.

Yager, R. R., et al. 1987. *Fuzzy Sets and Applications: Selected Papers by L. A. Zadeh*. New York: Wiley.

Yancey, Philip. 1995. *The Jesus I Never Knew*. Grand Rapids: Zondervan.

————. 2000. "Living with Furious Opposites." *Christianity Today* 44.10: 70–81.

Yoder, John H. 1972. *The Politics of Jesus*. Grand Rapids: Eerdmans.

Zadeh, Lofti Asker. 1965. "Fuzzy Sets." *Information and Control* 8:338–53.

Index